Understanding Waldorf Education

Dedication

For my wife, Carol, who has taught me so much *from the inside out.*

Acknowledgments

This book was made possible through the efforts of Richard Ailes, Barbara Bedingfield, the late Colonel Edward Imperato, and the generosity of Phyllis Norman. It was their foresight and their steadfast support and funding that made this project happen.

Many individuals helped to shape the educational ideas in this book, foremost among them, John Gardner, Lee Lecraw, and Sheldon Staff from the Waldorf Institute at Adelphi University, who provided me with a firm foundation in Waldorf education and helped me to understand what it takes to be a teacher. I thank them for setting the bar so high.

In addition there are my friends and colleagues at the Washington Waldorf School and, of course, my students who taught me so much about teaching and about myself. I thank them for their hard work, their enthusiasm, and most of all, for their patience.

Lastly, I want to thank those who assisted me in writing this book:

My colleagues at the Nova Institute—Barbarina Heyerdahl and Bruce Libonn

My editors, Kathy Charner and Kate Kuhn, whose expertise and sensitivity are woven together perfectly

Jerilyn Ray-Shelley, for her devoted camera work and her watchful eye

E.F. Wen, for her beautiful border designs

Larry Conner and the Waldorf School of Baltimore for the photographs of some of their students

Vanessa and Tria Chang, Megin Charner, Charles Covey-Brandt, Emma Heirman, Sam Charner, and Ava Petrash for sharing examples of their work

And Chip Rood at Gryphon House, who is both friend and publisher

Understanding

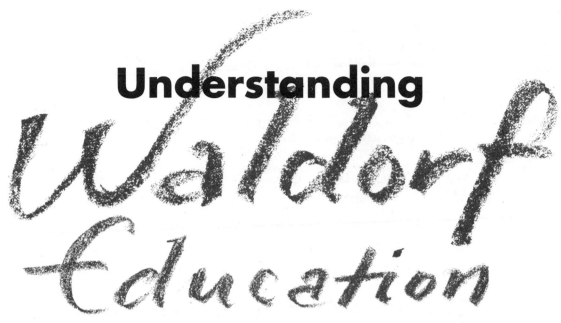

Waldorf Education

TEACHING FROM THE INSIDE OUT

Jack Petrash

gryphon house®, inc.

> The Nova Institute is a non-profit organization seeking to bring fresh insights into teacher education through a deeper understanding of children. (www.novainstitute.net)

Copyright © 2002 Nova Institute
Published by Gryphon House, Inc.
10726 Tucker Street, Beltsville, MD 20705
Visit us on the web at www.gryphonhouse.com

Illustrations: Tria Chang, Vanessa Chang, Megin Charner, Emma Heirman, Ava Petrash, Jack Petrash, and E.F. Wen
Photographs: Larry Canner and Jerilyn Ray-Shelley

Library of Congress Cataloging-in-Publication Data

Petrash, Jack, 1949-
   Understanding Waldorf education: teaching from the inside out / Jack Petrash
      p.cm
   Includes bibliographical references and index.
   ISBN 0-87659-246-9
   1. Waldorf method of education. I. Title.

   LB1029.W34 P48 2002
   371.39--dc21

                                                      2002023720

Bulk purchase
Gryphon House books are available for special premium and sales promotions as well as for fund-raising use. Special editions or book excerpts also can be created to specification. For details, contact the Director of Sales at the address or phone number on this page.

Disclaimer
The publisher and the author cannot be held responsible for injury, mishap, or damages incurred during the use of or because of the information in this book.

Table of Contents

Foreword

The secrets of Waldorf schooling are the prize we're after in spending time with Jack Petrash and his book, but oddly enough the best approach to Waldorf wisdom lies in first understanding the pedagogy of state schooling.

When Prussian one-size-fits-all schooling was brought to America in the middle of the 19th century by Horace Mann and others, this country had already been declared the best educated nation in history by the French essayist, Alexis DeTocqueville in his immortal classic, *Democracy in America*. The America he saw was a place of one- and two-room schools, a place where dozens and perhaps hundreds of schemes of education competed, drawing their strength from local traditions, local values, and citizen oversight, and the Prussian straightjacket was no part of this educational scene.

It's easy enough to hear about the excellent qualities of Waldorf education. Waldorf, invented by a Austrian philosophical genius named Rudolf Steiner, was first employed with the children of workers at the Waldorf-Astoria cigarette factory in Stuttgart, Germany after WWI in 1919. But the gulf between hearing of Waldorf and understanding it is vast. That's where the book you are holding comes in.

The Steiner philosophy that drives Waldorf education is a philosophy in which human possibility is seen as infinite. Whatever premises about human nature you start with when you establish a school, the articulation of the system that emerges will inevitably reinforce those premises. In a sense, the shape of any school reflects its social architect's deepest beliefs about humanity, and the best world possible.

Waldorf recognizes the genius in all and sets out quite deliberately to coax the muscles of that genius into play—in a far different fashion than the pedagogical orthodoxy, as you're about to learn.

My own experience with Waldorf-educated children is overwhelmingly positive. Although a public school teacher myself for 30 years, I've been fortunate enough as a public speaker on school reform to have been invited to lecture at Waldorf schools all over the country. What I've seen on these trips has been a revelation to me of what might be possible.

I could launch into a presentation of the actual method, but for the fact that Mr. Petrash has already done that in fine fashion. I think you'll find what he has to say illuminating. I know I did.

John Taylor Gatto,
Former New York State Teacher of the Year,
and author of:
Dumbing Us Down
A Different Kind of Teacher, and
The Underground History of American Education
www.johntaylorgatto.com

Introduction

Several years ago, the MacArthur Foundation awarded one of its prestigious "genius" grants to Deborah Meier, a New York City principal from the East Harlem School District. She was commended for making three striking innovations in her public school. First, she recognized that 45-minute classes were not conducive to learning and so she restructured her school's schedule to create double periods in an effort to intensify and deepen the educational process. Second, she saw that effective teaching could not take place in isolation. Consequently, she instituted a program of inter-curricula instruction, the kind that could allow music teachers to help teach history or art teachers to help teach science and where written composition could be used to teach mathematics. Third, she asked the faculty to be part of the decision-making that would create school policies that would directly affect the work in their classrooms.

Meier's ideas spawned innovations in schools across the country. The time was right for change. But these ideas were not new. Just as there were environmentalists long before the first Earth Day, Waldorf Schools had been using these three educational principles for more than 75 years. Why was Waldorf the best kept secret in education?

This book is an attempt to make the Waldorf approach more widely known and show how some of the most positive reforms occurring in schools today closely parallel the work that Rudolf Steiner began with the first Waldorf School in the early part of the 20th century. It is my hope, also, that this book will convey some of the fundamental principles of Waldorf education in language that is accessible so that parents, teachers, and future teachers will understand the essential aspects of this delightful, practical, and healthy approach to education.

CHAPTER ONE

Broadening Horizons

"Waldorf education places the development of the individual child in the focal point, convinced that the healthy individual is a prerequisite for a healthy society."
—The International Conference on Education of UNESCO

Third-grade students have arrived at school early on a Sunday morning. Their suitcases are being loaded onto a bus to take them on a five-day trip to a working dairy farm in upstate New York. On the farm they will help bring in the cows, muck the barn, gather the eggs, and experience a different way of living. This is an important event for the children. For many of them, it is the first time that they will be away from their parents. The students have been preparing for this trip for a long time, knowing that all of the third graders at this school go on the Farm Trip. It is a rite of passage, something that fills the students with anticipation and with a certain amount of anxiety.

Their teacher has also prepared them for this trip. Some of the most important instructions have focused on the meals that the children will eat at the farm. The children are told that they may be served foods that they may never have eaten before, and that they are expected (unless they have an allergic sensitivity) to *try some of everything.* This invariably means that many children must expand their culinary horizons. And they do. They will return home after their time at the farm and report to their parents that they have actually eaten lima beans or beets for the first time and "they were good," or that they ate the crust on the homemade whole wheat bread that they helped make—and liked it. Everyone is pleased—parents, teachers, and especially the children—when this occurs. The idea that children should broaden their horizons and "try some of everything" is an essential part of a Waldorf education.

In a similar manner, the Waldorf curriculum exposes students to a wide variety of subjects, encouraging them to develop in a well-balanced way as it helps children to overcome gender stereotypes and, at the same time, expand their individual interests. Girls and boys take woodwork and learn to knit and sew, and everyone plays a musical instrument. The gifted math student is asked to leave the safe confines of abstract thinking and to enter unfamiliar territory, finding emotional expression through painting and movement. At the same time, the artistically expressive student is asked to experience the clarity and predictability of trigonometry and calculus. Athletes are encouraged to be artistic and artists are encouraged to be athletic. This effort to complement students' natural abilities begins at an early age and continues throughout their time at a Waldorf school. It is encouraged by the curriculum and supported by the fundamental understanding that a child's strength should not become their weakness because of one-sided development.

All children have predilections, areas of strength where they are more comfortable and interested. These interests are important and can become pronounced at an early age. Such interests generally reflect unique talents. They usually are the areas where students will excel during their years of schooling and later in the workplace and should never be ignored. And yet, on a personal level, these strengths need to be "rounded off" and expanded to bring fullness and completion to an individual student's development. The active child, the one who confidently feels the power of her own ability and is willing to lead, needs to add *thoughtfulness* and *sensitivity to others* to become an integral part of the group. In short, this student needs to add something less intrinsic to her nature, something controlled, measured, reserved, something less impulsive.

On the other hand, the thoughtful observant child needs to add a measure of impulsiveness and energy to his demeanor, something that makes life risky and exciting, and will eventually make him feel fulfilled. Even though most children won't choose to put themselves in situations that encourage this type of personal growth, it is what they will need and want when they are adults, and it is what they will admire and appreciate in others. Waldorf schools serve as advocates for children by offering an educational program that promotes well-rounded development.

Doing the Right Thing

Efforts to lead children to fullness must invariably be concerned with helping children develop the ability to separate what they *feel* from what they *do*. Education should be based on the understanding that for young children their impulse for activity is intricately connected with their feelings. If a young child wants a toy, he often takes it regardless of whose toy it is. Similarly, if a young child doesn't feel like doing something, she will often just run away. Gradually through their education at home and at school, children learn that they can't do something (such as hit another child) just because they feel like it. They also learn that there are times when they have to do something (such as clean up their toys) even if they don't want to.

For better or for worse, this is an essential ingredient in maturity, a characteristic of responsibility. Most adults stopped asking themselves long ago whether they feel like going to work on Monday morning. Likewise, mothers and fathers don't ask themselves whether they feel like getting up to change a crying baby, or make lunches, or help with homework; they simply do it. If children are to grow up to be responsible adults, both in the workplace and in the home, schools and homes must assist this process by encouraging the development of self-discipline.

Self-discipline is the ability "to do the right thing." A key element that enables self-discipline to develop in a healthy way is the early formation of good habits, habits that become "second nature." When children are young, it is possible to develop these habits by providing good examples and consistent routines. This enables children to learn by doing and is preferable to the reminders and lectures that are often given to older children when these habits are not established early on. When a young child becomes accustomed to hanging his coat on a hook whenever he comes into school, it becomes a natural part of what is done for years. When children develop the habit of clearing their desk and putting things away before they go out, it is easier for them to do what is expected of them even when they are in a hurry. A child's capacity to do what he doesn't always feel like doing will convey to homework, music practice, family chores, and even to aspects of a job. The good practices that children establish at an early age through imitation and regular repetition pave the way for the development of maturity and self-discipline later.

Children need to be responsible and responsive, inwardly as well as outwardly. Students need good "soul" habits as well as good work habits. In short, they need to be emotionally responsive, both to their lessons and with their classmates and teachers. They should not be allowed to erect a wall of disinterest and refuse to make emotional contact with what they study. I recently visited a sixth-grade class and saw a quartet of boys who refused to allow what they were being taught to engage them emotionally. They were studying geology, but all of their efforts went into acting "cool." They faced the side of the room rather than the teacher and continually exchanged glances with each other. There was no way they would show any whole-hearted interest in the subject. This type of situation demands immediate attention, resolve, and creative teaching. Teachers must go out of their way to help students, particularly boys, to be emotionally responsible before they do something cruel and heartless (Pollack, 1999).

A child's inner, emotional life adds vibrancy and color to his or her experience of the world. When students bring heartfelt interest to their studies, knowledge comes alive. This conjunction of feeling and thinking makes students more receptive and perceptive and undoes their natural tendency toward self-involvement. Students begin their education with their feelings melded with what they do. During their time in school, their feelings must merge with what they think. When feelings connect strongly with ideas, idealism is born. Engendering thinking that is warm, vital, and creative is an important goal of a Waldorf education.

Measuring a Student's Progress

The students in a seventh-grade class have spent the last three weeks studying electricity. They are completing their block study with a test. As they are handed their exam, their eyes fall upon the first question.

1. You are a spy on a secret mission, sitting by a window in a dimly lit Italian restaurant near the Potomac River in Washington, DC. The table is set in front of you. Your salad has been served *with oil and vinegar dressing and your drink has arrived—mineral water in a tall glass with plenty of ice and a thick slice of lemon. You desperately need to signal your companions to rescue you, but all you have is a low-voltage light bulb and one 18-inch piece of insulated copper wire. Around your neck you have a thin silver chain and a silver medallion, and in your pocket you have lots of change: pennies, nickels, dimes, and quarters, and several $100 bills held in a silver money clip. Describe how you could use your light bulb to signal your friends without getting up from your seat.**

The best education is one that always expects children to be active thinkers and asks them to use their imaginations to produce assignments that show originality and effort and not just a recapitulation of facts.

Waldorf schools are concerned with the development of the whole child, both the inner aspects that are more qualitative and the outer aspects that are more quantifiable. During the course of their schooling, all students will need to master basic skills in math and language arts. These skills are measurable and important and yet, in and of themselves, they do not insure healthy development.

The recent intensification in the use of standardized tests as means of assessing children's educational progress is problematic by Waldorf standards because test scores generally present an incomplete picture of students' abilities. William Ayers, the

* What follows is an actual answer from one student who found a creative, though somewhat extravagant way to make a voltaic cell.
I would take the $100 bills and soak them in lemon juice. I would alternate quarters and pennies and put pieces of the $100 bills in between the coins. Then I would take my silver chain and cut it in half with a knife and connect one half to one of the light bulb's terminals and the other half of the chain to the other terminal. Then I would connect one chain to the coin stack and tap the other end against the opposite side of the coin stack. The flickering light bulb would signal my rescuers.

author of *To Teach: A Teacher's Journey*, highlights the limitations of these tests: "The unfortunate fact is that standardized tests can't measure initiative, creativity, imagination, conceptual thinking, curiosity, effort, irony, judgment, commitment, nuance, good will, ethical reflection, or a host of other valuable attributes" (Ayers, 1993, p. 116).

Although the impulse behind standardized testing that seeks to make schools and teachers more accountable for the education of their students is well intended, it leans too heavily on one side of the brain and measures only a portion of human intelligence. This shortcoming is brought sharply into focus by Howard Gardner, the author of several books about multiple intelligences.

> Many observers are not happy with this state of affairs. There must be more to intelligence than short answers to short questions…

> But what if one were to let one's imagination wander freely, to consider the wider range of performances that are in fact valued throughout the world? Consider, for example, the twelve-year-old male Puluwat in the Caroline Islands, who has been selected by his elders to learn how to become a master sailor. Under the tutelage of master navigators, he will learn to combine knowledge of sailing, stars and geography so as to find his way around hundreds of islands. Consider the fifteen-year-old Iranian youth who has committed to heart the entire Koran and mastered the Arabic language. Now he is being sent to a holy city, to work closely for the next several years with an ayatollah, who will prepare him to be a teacher and religious leader. Or, consider the fourteen-year-old adolescent in Paris, who has learned how to program a computer and is beginning to compose works of music with the aid of a synthesizer.

> A moment's reflection reveals that each of these individuals is attaining a high level of competence in a challenging field and should by any reasonable definition of the term, be viewed as exhibiting intelligent behavior...Only if we expand and reformulate our view of what counts as human intellect will we be able to devise more appropriate ways of assessing it and more effective ways of educating it (Gardner, H., 1993, p. 4).

Howard Gardner's book, *Frames of Mind*, has helped to expand our appreciation of children's various abilities and has helped educators see that defining intelligence in narrow terms is counterproductive. According to Gardner, an approach to multiple intelligences (such as the Waldorf school's) assumes a position similar to that held in "classical times (when) it was common to differentiate between reason, will, and feeling" (Gardner, H., 1993, p. 7).

By evaluating children according to a three-dimensional paradigm, one that recognizes the importance of physical and emotional (intelligences) capacities as well as cognitive, Waldorf teachers apply the term *gifted and talented* to all children. It is a Waldorf teacher's responsibility to recognize each child's strength and, together with the parents, bring this strength to fullness through a well-rounded education.

For this reason, Waldorf teachers will assess children in a variety of ways to determine if they are developing a well-balanced array of abilities. The teachers will observe the children in various situations to see how they are progressing physically and emotionally, as well as academically. They will look for the signs of health: attentiveness, enthusiasm, involvement in class discussions, and interest. According to Eugene Schwartz, a well-known Waldorf educator and author, "the portfolio method of evaluation, which has rapidly gained acceptance among American educators, is more appropriate in regard to Waldorf methodology than are regular quizzes or standardized tests." Schwartz goes on to say that "teachers will consider things such as the child's drawings, paintings, knitting, facility of movement, musical skills, and oral expressiveness as no less important than the more easily determined powers of cognition and verbal memory" (Schwartz, 1992, p. 32).

These observations from a wide variety of subjects and situations are refined and distilled over the course of the school year. They provide a complete "portfolio" of a child's performance and progression throughout the year. They eventually become the essential ingredients in the annual written evaluation that is delivered each June. In this narrative, the teacher describes and characterizes the child's school performance rather than reducing it to a series of checks in boxes labeled "outstanding," "satisfactory," or "in need of improvement." Symptomatic episodes are recalled in the written report. Moments are described when the child's very best was evident. These descriptions are presented to the parents, and to the child as well, as an example of the ideal toward which the student can continually strive.

It was a busy morning and the entire first grade was astir. As we passed out the books and took out our crayons, the talking grew noticeably louder. So much so that I had to stop writing on the blackboard and turn to face the class. When I did, I saw E. seated at her desk, working intently. She had already begun her assignment, completely focused on the task at hand. This was an experience of E. that I observed on many occasions this past year— she was invariably ready and eager to work.

Waldorf teachers describe, first and foremost, what a child does well and always mention with appreciation the overcoming of difficulties and the development of any new capacity.

I was so pleased with C.'s accomplishments in grade eight. As usual, his work in math and science was exceptional. However, the moment when I was completely surprised and duly impressed by his performance was during our class' production of the musical version of Narnia. Both his singing and his acting were noteworthy. His self-assured and humorous manner in Act One helped our play start with the right mood and intensity as he set an example for the other members of the cast on how to speak slowly and sing loudly. It was wonderful to observe C.'s presence of mind, his hard work, and his determined effort to overcome his uncertainty and do a good job.

In addition, teachers mention areas where children need to make more progress. All students have places where further improvement is necessary. It is a teacher's responsibility to mention those aspects as well. This can be presented as a wish list, a hope for something that will be accomplished in the future. And when suggestions for overcoming weakness are presented in conjunction with the recognition of strengths, they are always easier to accept.

In fifth grade, L. wrote some of the most interesting compositions in our class. Her assignments were always lengthy and expressive. Because L. is an avid reader, she has an extensive vocabulary that she utilizes to make her compositions sound like written work done by an older student. However, there were times when I found myself unable to read all of the words on the page and that disappointed me. It is my hope that L. will take the time to write more neatly next year. If she were to do this, the other students and I would be able to enjoy her fine written work even more.

The Journey Toward Wholeness

Children and teachers need to work together on the journey toward wholeness. For this to happen students must feel that what is being asked of them is for their good, that these suggestions are not born of annoyance or crankiness, but out of care and concern for their future development. When students sense that their teachers see their best, they will assist rather than resist the process.

Educators should prepare children for life, not just graduate school or future employment. Teachers should be concerned with children's human development and with children's ability to give their own lives direction.

Recently, a mother of a former student told me how much she appreciated a conversation we had about 10 years ago, when her son was in my math class in eighth grade. He was an exceptional student in math and mastered any work that was given him. She wondered, at the time, if he should go to another high school, one that would offer greater specialization and allow his mathematical interests and abilities to develop in a more pronounced way.

She recalled how in the course of that conversation I had encouraged her to consider his emotional and active development as well, and this made sense to her. Her son remained at our school, worked with his hands, played well on the soccer team, was surprisingly good in dramatic productions, and still earned a perfect score on the math section of his Scholastic Aptitude Test (SAT). He is now a doctoral candidate in mathematics at the University of Texas. What was clear to his mother was that he was a better person because of the fullness of his education and in the process, his extraordinary mathematical ability continued to flourish.

Stories such as this provide the confirmation that teachers and parents need. When you work to prepare children for life, you can't tell if you're doing a good job right away. Children are riddles. Who they long to become is only revealed little by little during their educational journey. That is why Waldorf teachers often turn to inspirational verses to remind them of the ineffable mystery that is each child. The following verse by Rudolf Steiner, the founder of the Waldorf School movement, was given to the teachers of the first Waldorf school more than 80 years ago.

> Receive the children with reverence.
> Educate them in love.
> Send them forth in freedom.
> —Rudolf Steiner

References

Ayers, W. (1993). *To teach: The journey of a teacher*. New York: Teachers College Press.

Gardner, H. (2000). *The disciplined mind: Beyond facts and standardized tests, the K-12 education that every child deserves.* New York: Penguin Books.

Gardner, H. (1993). *Frames of mind: The theory of multiple intelligences*. New York: Basic Books.

Pollack, W. (1999). *Real boys: Rescuing our sons from the myths of boyhood*. New York: Henry Holt.

Schwartz, E. (1992). Holistic assessment in the Waldorf school. *Holistic Education Review*, 5 (4), 31-37.

CHAPTER TWO

Head, Heart, and Hands

"Education is not the filling of a pail, but the lighting of a fire."

—William Butler Yeats

Ain't Misbehavin'

Some students fidget. Their hands look for something to manipulate—a pencil, an eraser, a piece of paper, anything. Elaborate events can take place on a desktop with minimal equipment. I have seen students entertain themselves with only their fingers; they check their double-jointedness, bend every finger and crack every knuckle. Still others are more exuberant. If a lesson continues without some sanctioned activity, they will not be still. Their legs begin to move and their knees begin to rock the desk. Feet and elbows begin to explore boundaries, encounter neighbors, make incursions, and defend territories. But all of these behaviors (or as they are often termed, misbehaviors) have one common message for the teacher. These children are longing to be actively engaged in their lessons.

Maybe you were this kind of student. Or perhaps you were more inwardly active, a quiet student who sat still, and then turned away slowly and inconspicuously. And while you stared out into the distance, your imagination got the better of you and you were gone—off to another land, a land more colorful and adventurous than what your teacher was offering. You traveled to a place brimming with emotion, full of peril, intrigue, and romance. Whether you entered this world of imagination by gazing out of the window or by drawing on your loose-leaf paper or on your desk, you were expressing a strong urge—a desire to be engaged through the richness of your feelings.

There is another type of student, the one who furtively opens a book inside the desk. While the teacher is reviewing a subject of little interest, the child reads. This student is expressing a fervent desire to learn something new each day and is committed to doing so, even if it means "tuning out" the teacher. If an uninspired lesson does not engage this student's capacity to think and learn, an irrepressible urge takes over and the child will teach him or herself.

Rudolf Steiner designed Waldorf Education around the simple idea that children have within them three fundamental forces impelling them toward physical, emotional, and mental activity. As a teacher I have always appreciated that these three capacities were called *forces*. This reminded me continually that if I did not recognize my students' need to be engaged in these three ways, these three significant tendencies would *force* themselves on my attention in less appropriate ways.

Understanding that children need to be engaged in these three distinct ways, through head, heart, and hands, forms the primary educational paradigm at a Waldorf school. Rather than focus the educational work solely around the objective of acquiring knowledge, creating a meaningful learning process itself becomes the focus. Through multi-faceted, multi-sensory learning experiences, teachers and students use a variety of intelligences to develop three distinct capacities—for thinking, for feeling, and for intentional, purposeful activity.

Capacities for the Future

It is impossible to predict what the world will be like in 20 years or to foresee how best to prepare children for that time. Likely, the world that today's children will inherit will be even more complex and problematic. If intelligence alone could solve these problems, then well-meaning government officials already would have been able to effect positive change. If having more information were the answer, then we who live in the information age would have found a solution.

To be properly prepared, students are going to need more than an education designed to promote cognitive ability and the acquisition of information. Today's children will need three distinct capacities to meet the challenges of tomorrow's world. They will need to develop *imaginative thinking,* a thinking that enables them to perceive events with clarity, comprehend situations fully, and then to envision new solutions for seemingly unsolvable problems. They will also need a capacity for *emotional involvement* that is both sensitive and resilient so they will be strong enough to weather the inevitable emotional storms that will arise and yet sensitive enough to look beyond the obvious and to hear what is not spoken. Furthermore, children will need the capacity for *resolute determination* so that they can take their hopes and dreams and turn them into reality. These three capacities for *thinking, feeling,* and for focused, intentional activity, which I will call *willing,* are the best tools for an uncertain future.

Developing Thinking

When I was a child, I received the *Weekly Reader* in school regularly. I remember sitting at my desk and looking at a photograph of a firefighter dressed in a cumbersome white suit. The title of the article stated something about "The Miracle Fiber of the Future" and then went on to instruct young readers about the benefits of asbestos. Forty years ago,

Americans were so enthusiastic about asbestos that we put it in our floor tiles, our ceiling tiles, and our house shingles. We wrapped this friable carcinogen around our heating pipes in the basement and placed it in other strategic places in our homes, schools, and businesses. Today we are spending millions of dollars for its removal.

This is the obvious flaw in fact-based instruction. Whether we were taught about the solar system, the Soviet Union, or computers, much of what we had to learn in school is now outdated. Given the fact that the world is changing even more rapidly today, what can we focus on in education that will prepare our students for the unpredictable world they will inherit?

Wide-awake, perceptive observation is what our students need for the future. The ability to observe individuals, events, and the natural world more completely will promote both lively intelligence and interest. Children who know the world in this more intimate way, a type of knowing that reveals tendencies and patterns, that gives rise to questions rather than answers, and that embraces complexity, view knowledge as a by-product of an ongoing process, rather than an end-product of a finished deed.

For instance, all alphabets contain elements of straight and curved lines, and yet these elements have come together in extraordinary ways over the centuries to produce distinctly beautiful lettering styles. When middle school students investigate these different alphabets they can see so many ways that an alphabet reflects the culture and the times out of which it arose. In the medieval gothic capital letters (see example on the next page), students find evidence of pageantry and courtly excess. In the closely placed small letters, they see similarities with the tightly formed medieval cities and the tightly bound medieval mind. In the way that the letters are shaped, they can see hints of the portcullis gate that barred the way to a castle's entrance. And when the students write these letters they can feel how the endless repetition of small strokes was similar to the building of the great cathedrals stone by stone over long periods of time.

Gothic Calligraphy

This type of awareness is the starting point. It is a wakeful and patient presence of mind, a prerequisite for problem solving, a habit of mind that enables students to see much in a little and to read more than just books, a subtle ability they will definitely need. Tomorrow's problems will not be solved by choosing either *a, b, c,* or *d* on a multiple choice test, unless, of course, *d* simply notes—*none of the above* or *all of the above ...and more.*

To be prepared for the future, thinking will need to be imaginative and participatory. It will require that students not only discover the unknown answer to a problem, but also the question that is still waiting to be asked. Eventually, imaginative thinking will help them to envision many different solutions to the problems they encounter. And then they will need to reflect and consider the solution that will be best for everyone.

Developing Feeling

Educating students to be emotionally responsive and responsible requires the education of feelings. Schools need to teach these lessons as well, and this means recognizing the importance of a child's inner world. Educator James Higgins stated this aptly in his book, *Beyond Words.*

> If one could ask a tree which of its two worlds was the more real—the world above ground, of leaves, blossoms, and sunlight; or that below the ground, where the taproot

reaches for who-knows-what—what would it tell us? For those who understand the tree's message, it clearly states that there is no reality for one "world" without the other. What is a tree without a taproot? What is a taproot without a tree?

Communication between the two "worlds" of the tree, so necessary for mutual growth and development, is a private inner process. Dirt cannot be sprinkled on a leaf to nourish it; direct sunlight will not benefit a root. Only the tree itself, through its own mysteries, can convey the nourishment of one distant "world" to the farthest reaches of the other (Higgins, 1970, p. 87).*

While a child's emotional life may be mysterious and hidden, it still falls within the province of education. For years teachers have educated students' feeling life tacitly and unconsciously, through intonation, facial expressions, and through the books that they chose. This is no longer sufficient. It is imperative that education directly touch the hearts of children, to help them care about their fellow human beings and reassure them that there is beauty and goodness in this world and that they play a role in preserving that beauty and goodness. As Vaclav Havel, democratic leader of the Czech Republic, stated so poignantly in his address to the United Nations shortly after the fall of the Soviet Union in 1991: "The salvation of this human world lies nowhere else than in the human heart, in the human power to reflect, in human meekness, and in human responsibility."

To develop the capacity for emotional involvement, Waldorf schools enhance their educational program by integrating the arts throughout the curriculum. Artistic activities such as painting, drawing, drama, and music infuse every child's school experience. For example, when students are asked to produce a play out of their study of history, their feeling for a time period deepens. While making sets, gathering costumes, and learning lines, the students are transported into a particular era and become invested in the learning process. By fostering a heartfelt connection between the student and the subject, education becomes more meaningful, and also more memorable.

Photograph by Jerilyn Ray-Shelley

Developing Willing

When students come to know the world through thoughtful attentiveness and to know themselves through their emotional and creative responses, they have a more complete sense of what they want to do with their lives. The ability to implement intentions and do what you put your mind to requires resolve, discipline, and a sense of purpose. It creates an attitude that engenders confidence and fosters self-esteem. In a Waldorf school this is called *will,* and it is the third capacity that the schools seek to develop. It is related to self-directed activity and harnessed energy—action with purpose, focus, and intention. It is a key ingredient in self-determination and a vital component of strong character, and certainly a capacity that children will need to chart their own course in a complex and confusing world.

If our children are going to help change this world, they will need a reservoir of strength that is not stymied by obstacles. Children must believe that one person can still make a difference, and the power to make a difference is in the will. This term has many names—vitality, volition, vigor, vivacity. It is determination and perseverance that is unwavering. It is, as radio personality Garrison Keillor says, "the strength to get up and do what needs to be done." And it is exactly what our children need for the future. Without strength of will, our children's hopes and dreams will not translate into action.

Children develop will over time through conscious repetition and a gentle insistence on good habits. When the simplest tasks, such as pushing in a chair, playing musical scales, or sharpening a pencil become a conscious discipline, children are able to perform the mundane tasks that are at the foundation of success, whether it be academic, artistic, or athletic.

Three Stages of Childhood

Although the capacities for thoughtfulness, emotional involvement, and intentional activity are inextricably connected, they do not develop uniformly. Rather, they develop in pronounced ways during three distinct seven-year stages of childhood, and therefore, are worked with differently in preschool, grade school (grades 1-8), and high school.

Preschool

In early childhood, from birth until around the age of seven, the young child is primarily *active*. This is evident in the kicking legs of a crying infant and in the curling toes of a nursing newborn, and it is definitely experienced by any parent or childcare provider who tries to keep pace with a toddler. This urge for activity is also observed in the exuberant and purposeful play of the kindergarten child. It is through activity that the young child is most easily engaged and most easily taught.

Grade School

Needless to say, the urge to be active does not disappear when a child enters first grade; neither is the young child unemotional before this point. Rather, activity recedes in importance over time and is gradually supplanted by a growing inwardness during the grade school years. Over the course of the second phase of childhood, from the age of 6 or 7 until around the age of 14, feelings become paramount. This change occurs gradually, the way one season changes to another. A growing emotional capacity begins to show itself the way that the warm days of summer precede the solstice. And these changes come in waves, just like the stretches of crisp autumn weather that can arrive in late August, become more common by September, and then commonplace by Halloween.

High School

The third seven-year phase of childhood is the one in which thinking prevails. Teenagers are certainly emotional and active (when they want to be), but their capacity for critical thinking shows itself in a pronounced way with the onset of adolescence and particularly at the beginning of high school.

The Balanced Development of All Three Key Capacities

In Waldorf schools no single capacity is viewed as more important than another. To foster a child's healthy development, we need to encourage a balanced growth of all three aspects so that in the end, clear, insightful thinking will rest upon a strong foundation of purposeful activity as well as a framework of emotional development. This natural and healthy progression from active experience and emotional response to conceptual understanding is a basic tenet of Waldorf education. Author John Gardner pointed this out in his book, *Education in Search of the Spirit*. "The thoughts that have started in early childhood as active absorption into the environment, and gone on during the elementary years to become articulated feelings with and about things, flower at last as living ideas. These are the content of real intelligence" (Gardner, 1996, p. 73).

This view of child development is embraced as well by the Alliance for Childhood, an organization comprised of educators and physicians who are concerned about the plight of children across the world.

> Young children make the most dramatic strides, in terms of nearing their full adult potential, in their sensory and motor skills, and the neural regions most related to them. During the grade school years and beyond children continue to progress incrementally in motor and perceptual skills. But now the most dramatic gains are in their social and emotional skills. The brain regions most involved in emotion

near maturation as children refine their social skills and their capacity to regulate their own moods and behavior. Finally, after puberty, the developmental focus within the brain shifts to the regions of the brain that enable the most advanced thinking, relying upon abstractions and critical judgment. Also, a rich network of neural connections develops between these areas and brain regions most directly involved in emotion and movement (Cordes and Miller, 2000, p. 7).

The balanced development of these three capacities produces well-rounded individuals. Americans have long admired individuals who have displayed such diverse talents: The blending of thoughtfulness and practicality (or "handy-ness") in Thomas Edison; the merging of artistic sensitivity and keen scientific observation in George Washington Carver; or the physical resilience and intelligence of adventurous scholars such as Jane Goodall and scholar-athletes such as Bill Bradley. These exemplary individuals are models of overcoming one-sidedness, yet balance does not seem to be an important educational goal in our schools. Because Waldorf schools are committed to promoting this well-rounded three-dimensional view of child development, this idea exerts significant influence over the entire education.

Dimensions of the Day

This three-dimensional paradigm influences the structure of the day in a Waldorf school. For grade school and high school students, the day begins with an extended lesson lasting up to two hours. This is called "the main lesson"—the time when the students are called upon to be most attentive and thoughtful. During these intensive study times, students are asked to use their thinking in a concentrated manner. Students and teachers study main lesson subjects intensively for three weeks to four weeks, and then new subjects are taken up. These longer, more concentrated periods of study—often called block teaching—are growing in popularity in other schools as well. This approach that uses block teaching is "part of a quiet revolution taking place, school by school, in districts all over the country" (DeBrosse, 1997).

In contrast, the afternoon is viewed as a time when lessons requiring more activity, such as woodwork, crafts, art, and physical education, are scheduled. These classes enable the students to balance and replenish the stillness and focus of the early morning with busy hands and energetic movement. In the middle portion of the day, classes that engage the feelings— painting, singing, foreign language, eurhythmy, and form drawing—join the more traditional skills classes and take place from mid-morning to lunch.

Although the three-dimensional paradigm influences the work of the entire school, it is applied differently by the preschool, grade school, and high school teachers. These are more than differences in degree. In each separate phase the child's developmental needs require a singular approach and a unique program. In each area, the teachers work with their children in different developmentally appropriate ways. Their approach has been acquired through separate teacher training programs and refined through classroom experience. We will begin to explore these distinctions by looking at Waldorf preschools in the next chapter.

References

Cordes, C. & E. Miller. (2000, September 12). *Fool's gold: A critical look at computers in the classroom.* College Park, MD: Alliance for Childhood.

DeBrosse, J. (1997, August 4). Schools try longer classes, faster pace. *Chicago Sun Times*, 1B, 4B.

Gardner, J. F. (1996). *Education in search of the spirit.* Hudson, NY: Anthroposophic Press.

Higgins, J. (1970). *Beyond words: Mystical fancy in children's literature.* New York: Teachers College Press.

CHAPTER THREE

The Waldorf Preschool

"I am struck by the fact that the more slowly trees grow at first, the sounder they are at the core, and I think that the same is true of human beings. We do not wish to see children precocious, making great strides in their early years like sprouts, producing a soft and perishable timber, but better if they expand slowly at first, as if contending with difficulties, and so are solidified and perfected. Such trees continue to expand with nearly equal rapidity to extreme old age."
—Henry David Thoreau

A three-year-old boy is sitting quietly in the backseat of his father's car eating an apple. He looks down at the fruit in his hand and asks, "Daddy, why is my apple turning brown?" "Because after you ate the skin off, the meat of the apple came in contact with the air which caused it to oxidize thus changing its molecular structure and turning it into a different color." There was a long silence. Then the boy asked softly, "Daddy, are you talking to me?" (Cooke, 1988, p.93)

Accelerated learning has long been in vogue. When a third grader's reading ability is measured to be on a seventh-grade level, parents and teachers are pleased. When a seventh grader's mathematical ability is comparable to that of a tenth grader, there is cause for celebration. And when our high school students take advanced placement college courses, we assume that the situation could not be better. However, when we meet a 25-year-old who is too staid and predictable, we are not impressed. In reality, we do not like people to be "old" before their time, and yet our schools encourage this and pat themselves on the back when they succeed.

Running counter to the push for accelerated or "early" learning is our appreciation for youthful vitality. We value vibrancy and exuberance, characteristics of youthful individuals at all ages. Our task as educators, if we wish to preserve what we value, is to cultivate and nurture youthful vitality rather than promote premature aging. The key to this is to create school programs that value and protect childhood.

Throughout the last century, Waldorf schools around the world have been working to safeguard childhood. They have established an approach that lets children be children. Waldorf preschools have a lot in common with other excellent early childhood education classrooms, and brain research has underscored the fact that the Waldorf approach to education is based on a commonly accepted understanding of the developing child (Healy, 1990).

Scientific studies have shown that young children's brains have marked plasticity. This means that children's early experiences will affect brain structure by establishing complex or simplistic neural pathways. According to Rudolf Steiner, the founder of Waldorf schools, "as the muscles of the hand grow firm and strong through doing the work for which they are suited so the brain is guided into the correct course of development if it receives the proper impressions from the environment. The work of the imagination shapes and builds the forms of the brain" (Steiner, 1996, p. 19).

This statement of Rudolf Steiner's has been substantiated by the more recent work of Jane Healy. "What children do every day, the ways in which they decide to pay attention, shapes the brain. Not only does it change the ways in which the brain is used, but it also causes physical alterations in the neural wiring system" (Healy, 1990, p. 51). Clearly, the environment into which young children are placed matters. A classroom that is stimulating and yet protective, comforting, and safe is essential.

In the Waldorf preschool the students enter a room that looks more like a home than a classroom—part kitchen, part playroom. The lighting is subdued, the curtains and walls a delicate color, and the furniture simple and natural. Most toys and play structures are wood, and carpeting encourages children to find a place on the floor to play.

According to a recent article in the educational journal, *Encounter*: "Those involved in school reform are rethinking how learning environments should look and feel. Some, such as those interested in brain-based research, believe schools should resemble the home" (Hart, 1983; Jensen, 1997). Hart's research on brain-compatible learning environments, as well as Jensen's, has prompted certain educators to take a conscious look at the way "classrooms are arranged and decorated" (Goral and Chlebo, 2000).

In the Waldorf approach to working with young children, early academic instruction is absent. The pressure for early learning is one of the most significant factors affecting young children's experience today. Across the country there is an increased emphasis on direct instruction in the early years. The growing importance of test scores in the grades as a measure for determining academic success has compelled schools to begin academic instruction at an earlier age. It is now customary for reading and arithmetic to be taught to five-year-olds in kindergarten. The question that educators are beginning to ask is one that Waldorf educators have long been asking: "What is the price we pay for accelerating academic instruction?"

Although the Waldorf preschool provides young children an education that is rich in language experiences, sequential routines, and learning opportunities, it has a different objective. The children are placed in a learning environment that provides many *natural* opportunities for learning. If children learn to count or to memorize a song or a poem, it is out of their own impetus and occurs naturally when they are developmentally ready and not through direct instruction. The implicit understanding is that it is counter-productive to require participation in advanced activities at an early age. In fact, brain research has shown that early academic instruction can actually be harmful. Educational psychologist Jane Healy explains this in her book, *Endangered Minds: Why Children Don't Think.*

> Before brain regions are myelinated [and nerves have the outer coating needed to transmit impulses], they do not operate efficiently. For this reason, trying to make children master academic skills for which they do not have the requisite maturation may result in mixed-up patterns of learning. I would contend that much of today's academic failure results from academic expectations for which student's brains were not prepared—but which were bulldozed into them anyway (Healy, 1990, p. 67).

The Waldorf approach to early childhood education raises a crucial question. If teachers are concerned with children's proper brain development and yet reluctant to impose early academic instruction, what types of activities should they incorporate to "guide the brain in its correct course of development"? The answer is simple: young children will learn by doing. And what young children love to do most is play.

The Importance of Play

Out on the playground at recess a teacher approaches one of her students. He is digging a hole with a large stick in the middle of the playground. His intensity, the large stick, and the hole placed where other children run and play have all caught the teacher's attention. She walks up to him and asks, "What are you doing?"
" I am letting the fire out," the child replies.
"Fire?" the teacher asks.
"Yes." The boy replies. "There's fire under the earth. I've seen it and I'm gonna let it out.
This child's imagination was captured by an experience of volcanic eruption and by the realization that under the surface of the earth there are great wells of molten rock that can burst forth in dramatic fashion.

Recently, the Smithsonian Institution in Washington, D.C. hosted a conference "to explore the role of play in the inventive process" and to demonstrate how "the creative processes of inventors, scientists, and artists often share striking similarities, including the manipulation of the physical world through play." During this conference presenters and attendees explored the role of playfulness in the lives of creative and inventive thinkers, such as Sir Alexander Fleming, who discovered penicillin when he drew colored pictures in his petri dishes. He was pleased and excited by a blue mold that he was able to grow and kept using it in his pictures. The discovery of the medical properties of this antibiotic came later.

In spite of the evidence that playfulness is a quality worth preserving, preschools across the country are reducing "playtime" and replacing it with more academic undertakings. A *New York Times* article stated, "The notion that kindergarten is a place where kids come and play is an anachronism…The increased focus on reading and math has come at the expense of play" (Zernike, 2000).

Tom Jambor, an expert in early childhood education, is one among many who raise concern about the movement away from playtime because it stands in sharp contrast to the needs of today's children.

> "Recess, once a reliable part of American children's school life, now is absent or only an afterthought in many schools… Once upon a time the vast majority of children came home from school and played in backyards and neighborhoods with friends. This supported the argument that children had plenty of time after school and on week-ends for play and the subsequent social experiences that promote total development. Today, however, too many children have restricted play experiences after school… Our children are at risk of losing their right to play. School recess (indoor as well as outdoor) is the best time for guaranteeing our children time to play" (Jambor, 1994, p. 17).

Play is a key component of the Waldorf early childhood program because it promotes well-rounded, three-dimensional development— engaging children emotionally, mentally, and actively.

Photograph by Jerilyn Ray-Shelley

Play develops emotional maturity through social interactions. When children play together, there is ample opportunity for socialization. According to *Play in the Lives of Children*, it is through play that "children move beyond their own egocentricity and expand their knowledge of the social world" (Rogers and

Sawyers, 1988, p. 64). By learning to share, to agree, and to cooperate, children learn how to be part of a social group. This understanding is essential for the formation of positive human relationships and is one of the important life lessons children begin to learn in a Waldorf preschool.

Another important benefit of play is the development of thoughtfulness and rapt attention. According to Joseph Chilton Pearce, a well-known author on human intelligence and creativity, "Play is the royal road to childhood happiness and adult brilliance... Children at play are not doing one thing with their hands or bodies, thinking something else in their minds, and speaking something else with their voice as we adults tend to do. They are totally absorbed in their play-world, absolutely one with their talk of play...Through this discipline, true concentration and one-pointedness develop" (Pearce, 1993).

Photograph by Larry Canner

Not only does play help to develop a child's attention span (an area of great concern today) it also gives rise to imaginative and divergent thinking, enabling children to consider situations and to solve problems in a variety of different ways.

Divergent thinking is a capacity that is essential for problem solving, an invaluable skill in today's fast-changing, high-tech world. Contrary to convergent thinking, which seeks a single answer for a single problem, divergent thinking looks for a multiplicity of solutions. Waldorf preschool teachers purposely choose play objects for the classroom that are not designed for a single purpose, but rather serve children in multiple ways. Nancy Foster, an experienced Waldorf preschool teacher, notes that "a curved piece of wood, for example, may be used as a bridge, or as a telephone, a boat, a cradle, a delivery truck, a fish, merchandise for a store, a package for a mailman to deliver, and so on. Younger children, of course, may see it as just another piece of 'firewood' for the 'fires' they love to build by piling up every movable object in the room" (Foster, 1999).

Children who are encouraged to play with the same object in a number of different ways develop the kind of flexible thinking that can consider a problem from a number of different perspectives.

Active Play: Indoors and Out

A teacher is standing near a gigantic tree stump on the playground. She is joined by three of the most active children and yet they are transfixed. She is holding a large brace and bit hand drill and a four-foot piece of closet pole. Together she and the children drill a hole in the middle of the stump and get ready to set the pole upright in the hole. But first they affix a pulley to the pole, slide a cord through it, and attach a red cloth to the cord with two small clothespins. Now the three children stand on the large stump, set the pole in place, and raise the flag for their ship, staring out over an imaginary sea, ready for adventure.

The third beneficial aspect of play is activity. A fundamental principle of early childhood education is that young children learn about the world most readily by interacting with their environment (Davey, 1999). This playful activity is encouraged both within the classroom and outdoors.

Outdoor playtime is a regular part of the Waldorf preschool program regardless of the season, which fosters an appreciation for the natural world. Even in urban settings, schools try hard to find protected natural play spaces with trees, bushes, a few tree stumps, and even an occasional mound of wood chips for the children to climb on. Black-topped areas and manufactured climbing structures, often features of a grade school play area, are passed up for more natural landscapes that foster imaginative involvement and a greater connection with the Earth.

When the children are out of doors, nature can provide the toys. Bark from the trees can be made into bark boats that float in a puddle. Pieces of moss can be gathered and used to cover the floor of homes that the children build in the hollows of tree roots and then adorn with acorns and other tree "droppings." Colored leaves in autumn and dandelions in the spring are woven into crowns that are worn by the children. All of these tiny constructions promote the fine motor skill of dexterity through delicate finger movements.

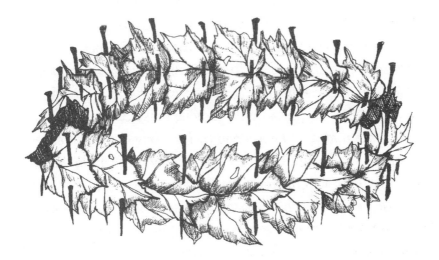

Vigorous outdoor play also gives the children a connection with nature. A fallen tree can be a play structure that encourages a wide variety of imaginary activities. Boys and girls will climb upon the "back" of this tree and imagine that they are riding on a whale or sitting in a school bus. On warmer days the children will nestle themselves in the shadow of this tree, close their eyes, and make the sound of a rocket ship, roaring off into outer space. And this is only the beginning of play that will continue for days, with children picking up the next day where they left off the day before.

An imaginative teacher can make it possible for the same kind of robust play to take place within the classroom in an orderly manner. Tree stumps and wooden play stands are standard equipment in the Waldorf preschool, equipment that children move around to erect elaborate play structures.

The door opens and a lively, wiry boy walks in. He greets his teacher and the other children, and places his jacket in the cubby. He is one of the older children in this non-graded classroom setting, and his play is naturally more focused and directed.

The young boy immediately walks off in search of building equipment. He gathers the playstands that are not in use, pushes several large stumps into position, and begins to erect a large play structure in this unoccupied corner of the room. This child is physically engaged—lifting, carrying, pushing, and arranging. He is thoughtfully involved, as well, moving these objects into place in a manner that was determined by him long before he entered the room. And clearly, he is wholeheartedly involved in what he is doing. The other children watch at first, the way that Mark Twain described the children watching Tom Sawyer whitewash the fence. Few actions are as compelling as work done with enthusiasm.

Play is serious business for children, as important for them as work is for adults.

The Importance of Work

Work also plays an important role in the Waldorf preschool, and teachers intentionally work in the presence of the children and, whenever possible, with their help. Important jobs have their place in the calendar of the week. There is generally a day for baking, a day to make soup or butter, a day to wash the placemats by hand, and a time every day to prepare the snack. The children participate in these activities because they long to knead, chop, and even to clean up. Participating in work enables the children to learn important lessons early on, lessons that are necessary for life. They learn to do their fair share and to help others.

Photograph by Jerilyn Ray-Shelley

Through the regular work of the classroom the children also develop a stronger connection with the real world. Some children are in danger of slipping into a "virtual" world where food and other everyday items just seem to appear. It is good for children to experience that bread is actually the result of someone's work, that it comes from stalks of wheat that are threshed (even on occasion in the classroom) from grain that is often ground in the classroom, and then from flour that they help mix with water and yeast and knead. They smell it as it bakes, and of course, they eat it when it is done. This gives children a complete understanding of where bread comes from. When the eating of this bread is preceded by a grace, a common practice in Waldorf schools, the mood is permeated with the right kind of awareness, an appreciation of all that is given to us here on the Earth.

> The silver rain, the shining sun,
> The fields where scarlet poppies run,
> And all the ripples of the wheat
> Are in the bread that we do eat.
> So when we sit for every meal
> And say a grace we often feel
> That we are eating rain and sun
> And fields where scarlet poppies run.
> —Anonymous

The Importance of Imitation

In addition to all of the positive benefits that work provides for children, there is one factor that is a crucial aspect of the work done in the Waldorf preschool. Meaningful and purposeful activity done in the presence of young children also provides them with actions to imitate, an irrepressible urge in young children. It is through imitation that young children learn most of the time.

Young children imitate far more than we imagine, and the impressions that they take in and mimic become behaviors that are learned for life. The role of imitation is essential when it comes to learning language; children master the complexities of their native tongue simply through experience and imitation. In a short time, children can learn a language effectively with all the subtleties of syntax and inflection simply by hearing the spoken word.

The reason that young children are able to learn so readily through imitation is because they experience the world with complete openness and without any reservation. They proceed from the basic assumption that the world is good. It is as though they are incapable of delineating between actions that are worthy of imitation and those that are not. They are so impressionable that whatever is done in their presence becomes part of them. This places tremendous responsibility on the teachers and parents of young children.

Rudolf Steiner brings the importance of imitation into focus: "Two magic words—imitation and example—indicate how children enter into a relationship with their environment. The Greek philosopher Aristotle called human beings the most imitative of creatures. For no age in life is this truer than for the first stage of childhood. It includes not just what happens around children in the material sense, but everything that can be perceived by their senses, that can work on the inner powers of children from the surrounding physical space. It includes all moral and immoral actions, all wise or foolish actions that children see" (Steiner, 1996, p. 18).*

For this reason, Waldorf preschool teachers try to act in ways that are worthy of imitation and at the same time instructive. Rather than admonishing children to speak softly or work carefully, teachers model these behaviors continually. It is

*Reprinted with permission by Anthroposophic Press.

through careful and conscious speech that children learn good diction and develop rich vocabularies as well as an appreciation for the beauty of language. It is by seeing their teacher place the lids back on the jars, return tools to their place, or wipe the counter clean and wash the dishes that children learn the proper sequencing for work activities and develop a sense of responsibility. All that takes place during the course of the day is potentially instructive to the young child. What matters most is a teacher's willingness to do things in the best possible way for the good of the children.

The Importance of Stories

Although the activities of play and purposeful work are central to the preschool child's experience, each day also has times of quiet reflection. Story time is a significant part of the program. Through told stories and puppet shows the children learn folk and fairy tales from around the world and develop literacy skills. Great attention is paid to the quality of speech and the choice of words in an effort to engage the children's imaginations. Stories are told from memory so that the magic of the spoken word, spiced with rhymes and little songs, can captivate the children, holding them spellbound, expanding both their vocabulary and their attention spans. These folk tales and fairy tales from around the world provide the children with models of good behavior without burdening them with admonishments or lectures. Story time is face-to-face contact when a storyteller creates the world of enchantment that children need and that nourishes them emotionally. At the same time, it prepares them for the academic work that they will encounter in grade school. Listening to stories can be an excellent preparation for school achievement as evident in this intriguing statement attributed to Albert Einstein: "If you want your children to be brilliant, tell them fairy tales. If you want them to be very brilliant, tell them even more fairy tales."

In addition to stories, preschool children come together each morning for circle time. Both the teacher and the assistant teacher, a common arrangement, stand together in a ring with the children and lead them in song and movement games, such as singing and skipping to folk songs. Learning is implicit in these activities, but "concealed" by the pure joy of participation. Hand-and-foot coordination, eye-and-hand coordination, a sense of rhythm, tonal awareness, spatial awareness, and a whole variety of intelligences are cultivated through enjoyable activity, making learning so pleasant that it is hard to tell that it is taking place.

Often preschools, kindergartens, and nursery schools are seen as places where learning is cultivated and where children blossom. Waldorf schools would welcome this association. These early years are all about the task of turning the soil of childhood and enriching it through active work and play. It is the time when the rich loam of childhood is kept friable through the power of imagination, a time when the first seeds of learning are warmed in a protected and loving environment. Waldorf teachers exhibit the patience of gardeners, taking a long view of education. They believe that when the seeds of learning are sown in fertile soil and tender shoots emerge, there will be a rich harvest when all bears fruit at the end of a long growing season.

The important work of Waldorf preschool teachers enables young children to begin to develop in significant ways the capacities that they will need for the future.

References

Cooke, S. (December, 1988). *Reader's digest*. Pleasantville, NY: Reader's Digest Association, Inc.

Davey, L.D. (1999). Play and teacher education. In M. Guddemi, T. Jambor, & A. Skrupskelis (Eds.), *Play in a changing society* (p. 42). Little Rock, AR: Southern Early Childhood Association.

Foster, N. (May, 1999). How do you choose toys and play materials for the classroom? *In a Nutshell*. Silver Spring, MD: Acorn Hill Children's Center.

Goral, M. & J. Chlebo. (2000). Where's Waldorf? *Encounter: Education for Meaning and Social Justice*, 13 (3), 43-52.

Hart, L. (1983). *Human brain and human learning*. New York: Longman.

Healy, J. (1990). *Endangered minds: Why children don't think.* New York: Touchstone.

Jambor, T. (Fall, 1994). School research and social development. *Dimensions of Early Learning*, p. 17-20.

Jensen, E. (1997). *Teaching with the brain in mind*. Alexandria, VA: ASCD.

Pearce, J.C. (Fall, 1993).Child's play. *Suncoast Waldorf Association: Teaching as an Art Newsletter*.

Rogers, C.S. & J.K. Sawyers. (1988). *Play in the lives of children.* Washington, DC: National Association for the Education of Young Children.

Steiner, R. (1996). *The education of the child and early lectures on education (a collection).* Hudson, NY: Anthroposophic Press.

Zernike, K. (2000, October 23). No time for napping in today's kindergarten. *New York Times*, p. A-1.

CHAPTER FOUR

The Waldorf Grade School*

"The greatest scientists are artists as well. Imagination is more important than knowledge. Knowledge is limited. Imagination circles the world."

—Albert Einstein

The desks have been pushed aside and two dozen first graders are moving in a circle in their classroom in a lively, yet organized, way. Their cheeks are flushed and their eyes are bright as they follow their teacher's lead, stamping, skipping, and singing together. Soon they pause, their feet still; they face the center of the circle and their arms begin to move. They are making the letter "S" in the air while they recite, "Sly and slinking serpents slither. Hissing through the softly stirring grass." These students are learning the letters of the alphabet in a variety of ways.

A three-dimensional approach to teaching infuses all of the educational work in grade school. Movement is an important part of each lesson as children learn to think on their feet as well as behind their desks. First graders begin each day by pushing their desks aside and creating a space for orderly, vigorous movement

---

* In Waldorf schools, grade school encompasses grades one through eight and grade school teachers remain with the same group of students throughout all eight years.

in the classroom. After they sing and skip and actively recite together, they reconfigure the room and sit, ready to learn. They are now glad to be restive and attend to the day's lesson. This vacillation between outer and inner activity allows the natural ebb and flow of children's attention. And when children turn their attention to their lesson, they should not be disappointed by dry teaching of abstractions. Grade school lessons must also touch the children's hearts and kindle their imaginations. This is certainly the case with the teaching of reading.

Teaching Reading

When the letter "S" was first introduced to the children through a dramatically told story about a snake, it was presented through an assortment of special words all included for their beauty as well as their phonetic relevance. The description of the elusive serpent helped the first graders to imagine the snake slithering, hissing, and sliding as it slipped to a secret, solitary spot to rest.

At the same time, the children could see a beautifully drawn picture of a snake on the blackboard. The image of the snake drawn to resemble the letter S, a modern hieroglyph, raises children's visual awareness, giving meaning to the new letter's shape. This is not the only letter taught in this way; all of the consonants in the alphabet are taught through a multi-sensory approach interweaving the spoken word with visual illustration.

> Waldorf schools do not waste much time debating the respective values of the sight and sound methods of reading. They use both, and more besides. But their uniqueness lies in the way they release the inherent power of the miraculous word from the humdrum of conventional speaking writing and reading.

> Thus letters… fill the room with sound, and will be put on paper with loving care, in color, using great strokes. They will be painted large with fantasy before being drawn small

in the conventional style. The shape of the B for instance, may be extracted from a bumblebee, or a butterfly, or a bear. This B retains in its form something of the burgeoning, blooming, bountiful things of which it speaks. The children quickly sense the relationship. They will do the walking, dancing, or modeling of B and the painting, drawing, and writing of a sense for the formative quality that lives both in its given shape and in its shaping sound (Gardner, 1996, p. 81).*

The first graders are involved actively through movement and through the work that they do each day in class. All of the letters of the alphabet are carefully drawn and written, accompanied by related words, and recorded in blank books or on large sheets of paper. The illustrations of the stories bring life and color to the text. In most Waldorf schools, the first grade children will even make their own readers. By allotting time for this work and by saving this work in bound books, the children are receiving an important message: What they do is of great importance. Throughout the eight years of grade school and into high school, Waldorf students make their own textbooks and work books. During each subject block (see pages 33-34 for an explanation of the block approach), students spend ample time writing the text and creating the illustrations to create these "main lesson" books.

This imaginative approach of teaching letters touches the hearts of the children. These varied language experiences help children become attuned to the qualitative aspects of language, fostering a subtle awareness of sound. The letters become familiar and are viewed fondly as acquaintances because they are related to characters in stories that the children enjoy.

For instance, the letter "K" is often introduced through the picture of a king, and the children are taught to look for the king's shape at the beginning of words that start with the "K" sound. Each year, however, first graders must also be brought to

*Reprinted with permission by Anthroposophic Press.

an understanding that the "K" sound can be made by the letter "C" as well. This can be a little confusing for new readers. It is here that imaginative stories can help.

Once the king was troubled. There was so much for him to do in his kingdom, but so little time. He needed a trusted helper, someone he could count on continually. But he didn't know whom to choose, for he was alone and had no queen to share the responsibilities of the kingdom. Should he choose his

daughter who was a continuous help in courtly matters? Should he choose the courageous knight who guarded his castle? Or should he choose his counselor whose consultations were always carefully conducted? Because he was at a loss, he traveled to the farthest corner of his kingdom to consult with the wise old crone who knew all of what was to come.

So he ventured all the day to her cottage where he consulted her about his concern. She looked carefully into her crystal ball for some time and then finally spoke. "Tonight when you return home, the first one to come to greet you will be your most trusted helper."

The king returned, but on the way it began to rain and this slowed his travels. When he arrived home, it was late and the castle was dark. All was still. His daughter had already gone to sleep and so had his knight and his counselor. At first he thought that the wise woman was wrong. There was no one to greet him. He stood warming himself by the last embers in the fireplace and was confused. Then suddenly, he felt something rub against the back of his leg and there was the castle cat standing near him. It was the castle cat that had come to help the king. And the cat brought the letter "C" to help the king. You see, children, there are times when you will hear the king's sound, but you will not see the king's letter "K". Instead you will see the cat's letter, the"C", and then you will know that the king is busy and the cat is being called on to help.

A story like this takes only an additional 10 minutes to tell, but it leaves a lasting impression and is much more suited to a child's understanding than to speak of etymology of certain words or to say that English is a confusing and difficult language to learn.

This story of the king can be taken further when other letters are introduced. I was once telling my children a whimsical story about a naughty child named "Noisy Nimmy," which I made up for them to introduce the letter "N" when I suddenly realized that an important secondary lesson was possible.

Nimmy was out in the woods being his normally noisy self, using his favorite words such as "No" and "Not" and "Never," when unexpectedly the king appeared with his entourage. Normally you would hope that a child would be quiet in the presence of the king, but oh no, not Nimmy. He was noisier than ever. The closer the king came, the noisier Nimmy grew. In fact, children, whenever you see Nimmy next to the king, you won't hear the king at all. Remember children, when you see words like KNOW

and KNIGHT and KNIFE where the K and the N are together, you
will only hear Nimmy, and the King will seem silent.

The following year, when my students were reading a story
together, they encountered the word "gnat" and one of them
said, "There's that noisy Nimmy, and look, you can't hear the
"G" at all. That Nimmy!" The story still lived in them and their
understanding just continued to grow.

This imaginative approach to teaching involves the whole
child—actively and emotionally, while they learn. Make no
mistake, this innovative multi-sensory instruction is not trivial. It
is based on a sound approach to education that leads students to
higher order thinking. Much is written about the different types
of learning experiences that utilize both sides of our brain.
Phonemic awareness is generally viewed as a left hemisphere
activity using our auditory and analytical capacities. Visual
learning is a right brain activity, particularly when meaning is
ascribed to a subject. In Jane Healy's book, *Endangered Minds*,
she writes that "all thinking, even language processing, calls
upon both hemispheres at the same time. The trick, in a well
functioning brain, is to mix and match the abilities of the two
hemispheres so that the most adaptive processing 'style' is
brought to bear on any learning situation. Since the hemispheres
carry on continual and rapid communication over the bridge of
fibers (corpus callosum) that connects them, their ability to
interact is probably the ultimate key to higher-level reasoning of
all kinds" (Healy, 1990, p. 125).

Communication between the left and right hemispheres of
the brain occurs when language instruction employs both
phonemic and visual awareness. "People who learn to read both
a letter-type and a picture-type script as, in Japan, tend to
process language more equally between the two sides of the
brain than do people who read only letter-type scripts" (Healy,
1990, p. 212).

The Waldorf approach to reading is taught in a multi-sensory way, using both dramatic visual images and the physical experience of the letter through walking and clay or beeswax modeling. It engages the whole child, using both sides of the brain and by doing so, makes learning to read more meaningful and more memorable, but also more rewarding.

Many Americans can read, but choose not to. To cultivate readers who are thoughtfully, emotionally, and actively engaged by the books that they read, we must teach children to read in a manner that activates them inwardly. Reading instruction needs to be imaginative, heartfelt, and lively so that it engages the whole child. Then it can become a fully human and fulfilling experience.

Teaching Through Art

Art plays a significant role in Waldorf Education. In his book, *The Kind of Schools We Need*, Eliott Eisner, professor of Education and Art at Stanford University, echoes the sentiments of many children:

> [A]rt—the visual arts—was a source of salvation for me in the two elementary schools I attended between five and thirteen years of age. I did not do well in elementary school: arithmetic was problematic and frustrating, my handwriting was and is at present not particularly good, spelling was a relentless bore, and English grammar—the diagramming of sentences whose features remain before me as vividly now as they were then—was largely meaningless, even when I was able to correctly indicate the difference between a direct and an indirect object. But art—ah, that was another story" (Eisner, 1998, p. 57).

I have seen how artistic activities help children to become emotionally engaged in the learning process. Emotional activity is an integral part of the Waldorf grade school experience.

Drawing, singing, painting, and poetry have their regular place in the educational program because they provide nourishment for the affective aspects of a child's development.

If physical activity in the preschool provides the foundation of support in the early years, emotional involvement in the grade school provides the framework upon which solid academic work will rest. "Evidence from the brain sciences and evolutionary psychology increasingly suggests that the arts (along with language and math) play an important role in brain development and maintenance" (Sylwester, 1998, p. 32).

The teaching of any subject, from science to history, can be enlivened and enhanced by incorporating art into the instruction. Roman History, a standard social studies subject taught to 11- and 12-year-olds, offers a wide variety of artistic experiences. The students can encounter poetry through the recitation of Lord Byron's *Ode to a Dying Gladiator,* or dramatic monologue via Mark Anthony's speech in Shakespeare's *Julius Caesar.* They can develop an appreciation for architecture with a free-hand pencil drawing of the Colosseum, and for calligraphy through the duplication of the stately Roman letters on the Emperor Trajan's column. And there are few students who need to be encouraged to depict a battle of the gladiators with crayons or colored pencils. All of this artistic involvement elicits an interest and responsiveness to subject matter that is counter to the normal diffidence generally expressed by so many 11- and 12-year-olds. These students' strong feelings are released in artistic expression, making their learning a whole-hearted activity.

Mathematics and Art

Teaching with an integrated curriculum approach, which is a common educational reform, is an important part of the Waldorf approach to education. Art is not merely taught in isolation as a separate subject. It is more often used in combination with other subjects to enhance the learning experience. This artistic involvement is possible with all subjects including math and science. For example, when sixth graders learn geometry in a Waldorf school, they learn it first through geometric drawing. The construction and division of circles, the bisecting of lines and angles, the constructing of perpendicular lines, all done with mechanical drawing equipment, enable the students to produce striking geometric designs while familiarizing themselves with properties of circles, polygons, and angles.

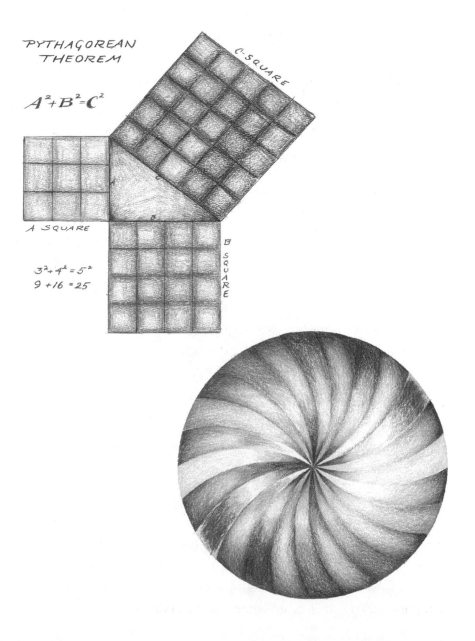

PYTHAGOREAN
THEOREM

$A^2 + B^2 = C^2$

C-SQUARE

A SQUARE

B SQUARE

$3^2 + 4^2 = 5^2$
$9 + 16 = 25$

Science and Art

Students long for lessons that will engage them emotionally. In grade seven, the study of combustion, a subject that immediately captures their attention, often begins with the candle. However familiar students may be with candles, when asked to describe a candle flame there is surprisingly little agreement among the students as to its color or composition.

A good place to begin a study of combustion is to ask the students to draw the candle's flame with exacting precision using colored pencils. This demands careful observation. The students will notice how the bottom part of the candle is dark and blue, how the pointed top of the candle's flame is intensely yellow, and how in between there is a less radiant orange.

"There is no better, there is no more open door by which you can enter the study of natural science by considering the phenomena of a candle."

Michael Faraday

Then the teacher can insert one end of a hollow glass tube into the dark part of the candle flame, and the other end into a test tube. In a few seconds a heavy, whitish vapor will be moving through the tube and collect in the test tube. Usually, the students respond emotionally to this observation with characteristic "oohs" and "ahs." When the vapor has been collected, the test tube is corked and placed in a bowl of ice. Within a few minutes, a white coating lines the inside of the bottom of the test tube.

The students are surprised by what they see and are generally a little puzzled that such a simple everyday phenomenon as a lighted candle can lead to such surprising results. Asking them to write down precisely what has occurred and to draw the apparatus used for the day's demonstration in accurate detail challenges their powers of observation—an important component of thinking. And as students draw their illustrations to accompany their written text in the main lesson books that they create (see Chapter Five, page 92, for additional information about main lesson books), they have time to reflect and speculate about the substance lining the bottom of the test tube.

The next morning, through a conversation with the students, it becomes evident that yesterday's demonstration showed the three physical states of matter: solid wax (the candle), liquid wax (the little pool at the base of the wick), and wax vapor (moving through the hollow tube). This understanding provides a good opportunity to demonstrate how physical change is different than chemical change.

When the candle is lighted again, the hollow glass tube is placed in the flame, this time higher up in the part of the flame that is bright yellow. Now a darker gas moves through the hollow tube and is collected in the test tube, corked, and placed in ice. After a time, however, this gaseous substance does not solidify to coat the test tube. The students have witnessed a chemical change. The collected gas is no longer wax vapor; now it is carbon dioxide, and the chemical reaction that formed the carbon dioxide gives the candle flame its light and heat. The students come to understand the essence of a chemical change and see its *irreversible* nature, how this substance, carbon dioxide, cannot be changed back into wax.

Now the students have begun to see the hidden laws that are behind these common, everyday phenomena. This allows the real educational opportunity to arise. If the students are now asked what in their own lives is irreversible, a serious discussion can occur with implications that may have an impact on a child's life outside of school. It is a combined sex-, drug-, and alcohol-education class, but the students don't see it coming, which allows for conversations that are authentic and spontaneous. In this way, students can begin to realize that the consequences for some of their actions (teenage sex, drunk driving, or drug use) can also be irreversible. This type of discussion does not inhibit a young person's understanding of a scientific concept such as chemical change, rather it cements that understanding with an emotional bond allowing learning to take place on a number of important levels.

The Grade School Curriculum

The Waldorf curriculum offers an organic structure that mirrors the developmental changes that take place over the grade school years. By being inwardly relevant, by resonating with a child's changing frame of mind, the subjects that are taught can meet their growing needs. Because a first grader's interests are markedly different than those of a teenager in the eighth grade, it is the task of each teacher to understand these interests and to teach to them *and through them*. Good teachers, in all schools, attempt to do this. Because the Waldorf curriculum was designed with this in mind, it can provide teachers with a head start by

giving them more direct access to the heart of childhood.
Key subjects reflect significant changes in the child's world. For
example, the introduction of local geography in grade four
comes at the very time when the 10-year-old's world is
expanding beyond the most familiar immediate surroundings.
Making maps of the neighborhood legitimizes a child's interest in
crossing boundaries. In a similar way, the sixth-grade math
curriculum mirrors the 12-year-old's prosaic interest in money,
purchases, discounts, sales tax, and tips and engages it through
the study of percents and simple interest in business math.
Seventh graders' preoccupation with their bodies is addressed
through the subject of health and hygiene. Suddenly, the study
of the skin, hair, and nutrition has immediacy. As with so many
things, timing is everything. The eighth-grade study of colonial
history comes when 13- and 14-year-olds are writing their own
inner "declaration of independence" and so the students have a
vested interest in the historical outcome. As Canadian educator
Kieran Egan writes in his book, *Imagination and Teaching*: "The
world is not objects out there; in as far as we can know the
world it is within us by means of that curiously reciprocal
arrangement whereby we also extend ourselves imaginatively
into it" (Egan, 1992, p. 60).

This understanding is an essential part of the Waldorf curriculum
and is even reflected in the stories that are told and read in the
classroom in the grade school.

The Role of Stories in the Curriculum

A story, particularly a told story, engages children completely. It
stills them outwardly and activates them inwardly, filling their
imaginations with pictures depicted in the telling of a tale. A
story also elicits a thoughtful response from the children. It
provides a model of organization, ordering information and
giving sequence to events, making it possible for learning to take
place effortlessly. And, of course, a story has additional value that

enables teachers to touch and instruct their students on the deepest level.

Photograph by Larry Canner

For centuries in all cultures around the world, stories have been used to instruct children on ethical and moral issues and to educate their character. This has been stated aptly by the well-known literary figure, Donald Murray, in his book, *Crafting a Life in Essay, Story, Poem*:

> Story allows us to bring order to experience, to find pattern in events, to discover meaning in confusion, and story allows us to share the order, pattern, and meaning. Through story we remember, understand, instruct, entertain, celebrate. The range of all human experience and the intellectual, emotional, and spiritual response, is held within the story. Stories contain and reveal our beliefs, our fears, our hopes, our knowledge of how the world works (Murray, 1996).

At a time when there is so much concern about the spiritual and psychological well-being of children, it is unfortunate that the story is underutilized in schools. Even the common fairy tale has important lessons to bring to children. When young children are told a fairy tale such as "Snow White and the Seven Dwarfs," they do not need to be reminded that envy is destructive. Envy is personified in the wicked queen and the children revile her from the start. They see past her superficial beauty and are repelled by her deceit and relentless ambition. The dwarfs, on the other hand, represent all that is simply and faithfully loyal. Their lonely vigil for the dead Snow White is touching. Their joy at the end is loyalty's just reward. Simple folk legends also have much to offer. They have heroes with character and spiritual strength such as Odysseus, Penelope, Rama, Sita, and El Cid, to balance the questionable pop stars, sports stars, and super heroes in current culture.

Each elementary grade at a Waldorf school has its story theme. These stories become the starting point for many language arts lessons. The children write their own synopses of the tales, extract dialogue for skits, work on plays and reports, spelling words, grammar lessons, even dictations. In grade one, the fairy tales are told. In grade two, the children hear fables, animal legends, and even stories about saints and beasts, such as St. Francis and the Wolf of Gubbio or St. Jerome and the Lion, where compassion for animals is pronounced. In grade three, the stories from the Hebrew Bible are told and in grade four, the Norse Myths and Native American stories. In grade five, the legends and myths of India, Egypt, Persia, and Greece move the students from story to history. Then in grades six, seven, and eight, stories and particularly biographies out of the history and geography curriculum are told.

The story is a many faceted jewel, and one of those facets is that it makes learning memorable at any age. When I was in public high school in New York City, I had a math teacher who had the unenviable assignment of instructing 25 tenth graders in geometry during the last period of the day. Needless to say, he had to work to get our attention, but he succeeded through the use of stories. On a warm, sunny, late spring afternoon he was preparing us for the state regents exam by telling us the tale of a Native American princess, *Sohcahtoa*. We had other things on our mind, but as he related the story of this lovely princess and her romantic inclination for a brave of her tribe, we were hooked. At the end of the tale, when he was sure that he had our attention, he told us that we should remember *Soh-Cah-Toa* because she would remind us that **S**ine = **O**pposite / **H**ypotenuse, **C**osine = **A**djacent / **H**ypotenuse and **T**angent = **O**pposite / **A**djacent. We groaned, of course, when we realized that we had been tricked into learning, but 35 years later I still haven't forgotten that lesson.

This teacher knew that the teaching of higher-level mathematics could be done effectively through stories. In Waldorf classes, fundamental math concepts are often introduced in the same way. In first and second grade, it is quite common to present the four mathematical processes as well as other key concepts through stories.

One day the king needed the help of one of his courtiers, Count Divide. Divide was the only one in the kingdom who understood how to keep things fair. If there were 12 rubies to be given away to 3 visiting dignitaries, Count Divide knew that each should get 4. And if 18 emeralds were to be given to the king's 3 daughters, then Count Divide knew that they should each receive 6.

Now it happened one day that the king was expecting visitors from another land and wished to give each of them a gift. He had 24 sapphires and would be receiving 8 guests, but he did not know how many jewels each guest should receive. He called for Count Divide, but he was nowhere to be found. He sent messengers out to scour the town, but they had no luck. Finally, he took matters into his own hands and went to Divide's house. Alas, no one was home.

When the king finally found Count Divide, he was beside himself. "Where have you been?" demanded the king. Divide said that he had been working in the mines. "Well," said the king, "What am I supposed to do when you are not around?"

"Oh," said Divide, "That is easy. Just go to my division house and put your bag of jewels inside the house so they are safe. Then leave me a note on the door to tell me how many guests are coming. And I will put the answer on the roof of my house so you will be able to see it from your castle."

In later grades, other important ideas and procedures in fractions, decimals, percents, and algebra can be brought forward in a similar way.

Science teaching is also enhanced through stories. Geology lessons, in particular, are enlivened through story telling. Relating the tale of the birth of Paricutin, a cinder cone volcano in Mexico, a teacher can bring a child to a captivating experience of the natural world. By describing an actual expedition to the subterranean lakes and rivers in the Yucatan, the students appreciate the mysterious aspects of our Earth, as well as an understand the striking contrast between the formation of igneous rock and the dissolution of limestone.

Regardless of the subject, stories can be used effectively when they are integrated into the curriculum. They are not used as a diversion, but rather as a time-tested method of instruction that is perfectly suited for the way children learn.

Stories that Heal

It was January of eighth grade and the students that I had taught from grade one were entering their final year in the grade school. It should have been a time of expectation and happiness, except a rift had developed in the class. A group of girls had become upset with the other girls in the class and the tensions and bad feelings were tangible.

These girls who had always been friends now ate lunch separately, sat apart in class, and went out to recess or off to the girls' room in separate groups. The situation was extremely uncomfortable, especially in the "family-like" atmosphere of our class, and seemed to be getting worse.

I was at a loss, and so I approached a more experienced colleague and asked him what he would do. He told me that he would look for a story, something that came out of the curriculum and was similar to the situation in the class. He said that he would simply tell the story to the students and then see if they could make the connection between the two events by themselves.

At the time, I was teaching world geography and after reading the day's newspaper, I decided to turn our attention to the Middle East. That previous day there had been a retaliatory early morning Israeli bombing raid on a Palestinian refugee camp in Lebanon in which six people had been killed, two of them children. So I told my students the story of that event, describing it from the perspective of the Palestinian refugees waking from sleep to the sound of planes and explosions, helping them through my words to imagine the confusion and the horror.

When I was done, the girls were obviously upset by the thought of the suffering, and one of them spoke up.

"Why can't they just get along. Why must they always fight?"

I tried tactfully to rephrase the question. "You mean why can't people who have lived next to each other for years live without hostility?"

"Yes," she said, "Why can't they?"

At that moment she and the other girls saw the parallel with their situation and the mood in the room changed. I didn't need to say anything. They made up shortly thereafter and from then on, they were friends again.

Learning to live with others is certainly a central lesson in a Waldorf school. Over the years that they are together, teachers help students to work out personal differences and difficulties. This is important and challenging work, the kind of work that will help children with their relationships later in life. Stories are invaluable in assisting with this effort because they make it possible for children to learn *from the inside out*.

The Role of Music in the Curriculum

Waldorf teachers weave together a variety of disciplines, including music, to make the learning experience rich and rewarding. This way of teaching, known as integrated curriculum, uses art to teach science, writing to teach math, and stories and literature to teach history and geography. Deborah Meier, whose work is mentioned in the introduction of this book, was awarded a MacArthur Foundation genius grant in education because of striking innovations in the program at her school in East Harlem School District. One of those innovations was the development of an integrated curriculum.

The following excerpt from *A Tree Grows in Brooklyn* by Betty Smith shows how imaginative, artistic teaching brings a child's school experience to life. Although it tells of a time over 80 years ago, music in schools is just as valuable today.

> "School was not all unrelieved grimness. There was a great glory lasting a half-hour each week when Mr. Morton came to Francie's room to teach music…He drew notes on the blackboard; he drew little legs on them to make them look as though they were running out of the scale. He'd make a flat note look like humpty-dumpty. A sharp note would rate a thin beet-like nose zooming off of it. All the while he'd burst into singing just as spontaneously as a bird.
>
> He taught them good music without letting them know it was good. He set his own words to the great classics and gave them simple names such as "Lullaby" and "Serenade" and "Street Song" and "Song for Sunshine Day." Their baby voices shrilled out in Handel's "Largo" and they knew it merely by the title of "Hymn". Little boys whistled part of Dvorak's New World Symphony as they played marbles. When asked the name of the song, they'd reply "Oh, 'Going Home'". They played potsy, humming "The Soldiers' Chorus" from Faust, which they called "Glory" (Smith, 1947, p. 161-162).*

*Reprinted by permission of HarperCollins Publishers Inc.

The vital role that music plays in education has also been underscored repeatedly in the cinema. Films such as *Fame*, *Mr. Holland's Opus*, and most recently, *Music of the Heart*, with Meryl Streep, draw attention to our common understanding that music enhances the school experience the way that few subjects can on their own. Music serves as a leaven in the school day, giving buoyancy and lightness to a lesson. And yet the value of music goes far beyond this enlivening.

In an issue of *Educational Leadership*, Norman Weinberger, a professor of psychobiology at the University of California at Irvine, wrote that "music has the ability to facilitate language acquisition, reading readiness, and general intellectual development, to foster positive attitudes and to lower truancy in middle and high school, to enhance creativity, and to promote social development, personality adjustment, and self worth." Music serves the student by engaging a wide range of capacities. Weinberger continues, "Learning and performing music actually exercises the brain—not merely by developing certain skills, but also by strengthening the synapses between brain cells. Brain scans taken during music show that virtually the entire cerebral cortex is active while musicians are playing" (Weinberger, 1998, p. 36, 38). Music is one of a number of subjects taught in Waldorf schools that effectively unifies the polarized tendency in children to be either expressively artistic or logically academic. Music leads to higher-order thinking by facilitating a combination of both.

In the elementary years, Waldorf students learn about music through two different types of teachers. There are music specialists who teach the students once or twice a week throughout the grades, offering singing and instrumental music classes, as well as chorus and orchestra. These teachers introduce the children to music theory, give them instruction and practice with singing, and see that each and every student receives basic instruction in playing a string instrument, either violin, viola, or cello.

In addition, the class teacher is responsible for teaching both the academic subjects and for introducing the study of music. This begins with the playing of a recorder in grade one. But a creative teacher will interweave the teaching of music into all areas of the curriculum. Music can even be incorporated into the teaching of arithmetic. I have heard children singing a *math song* to themselves while doing long division so they could remember the sequence of steps. Geography lessons about the United States come alive when children take a musical tour of the country, singing their way from California to Oklahoma, from New York, New York to the Erie Canal, and finishing with Woodie Guthrie's "This Land Is Your Land" or "America the Beautiful."

Science teaching can be enhanced through music, too. Sixth-grade students stretch their understanding of acoustics and their musical ability by filling a wide variety of glass bottles with varying amounts of water in an attempt to produce a musical scale and then to play an actual song. And many eighth graders have concluded their anatomy study of the skeleton with a rousing rendition of the gospel song, "Dem Bones, Dem Bones."

When music teaching is incorporated into the teaching of history, its benefits are even more pronounced. If students studying the civil rights movement in the United States or the anti-apartheid movement in South Africa can sing "We Shall Overcome" or "Siyahamba," they experience the passion and commitment that sustained the individuals who marched for human rights. The actual singing of a song enables the students to *feel* what it was like to be part of an important era in human history and this allows teaching to come alive.

Yet, Waldorf education is not simply about teaching art. It is about teaching all subjects artistically and creatively. *Education as an art* is the goal of every Waldorf teacher. It is not the easiest assignment, but it could be the most rewarding. It requires

Waldorf teachers, as well as students, to be inwardly active. It is this inner activity that will ultimately enable the class teacher to succeed.

The Waldorf Class Teacher

On the first day of the school year, the auditorium is filled to overflowing. The first graders enter as a class, and each child is carrying a flower. Once the children are settled, the new first grade teacher calls the name of each student. In this way this new class is introduced to the whole school. Each first grader stands when called, comes to the front of the auditorium, and hands a flower to the teacher. Roses, daisies, lilies, chrysanthemums, and lupines all fill a vase set on stage, forming a bouquet that serves as a metaphor for the formation of the class. This is the beginning. These children and their teacher will be together for the next eight years of elementary school.

Photograph by Jerilyn Ray-Shelley

In Waldorf Schools, the "class teacher," who will teach a class of students from first grade to eighth grade, accepts extensive and extended responsibility for the children as their main instructor. When strong emotional ties fostered by continuity develop between student and teacher over a long period of time, learning is furthered. To maximize this emotional connection, Waldorf schools place one teacher and a specific group of children together for the entire elementary school period.

Having a teacher remain with the same children for a number of years, which is a key component of Waldorf schools, is not new and is currently in use in public schools in the United States, Canada, Scandinavia, China, Taiwan, and Japan. This practice is called "cycling," "teacher-student progression," or more often, "looping," and has been experiencing a renaissance in schools. In most instances, teachers who "loop" stay with the same children for two years, but in Montessori schools, teachers have commonly remained with their students for three. "Looping," said New Hampshire educator Jim Grant, who coined the term 10 years ago, "is catching on like wildfire across the country. Suddenly teachers have realized that the best-kept secret is long-term relationships over time" (Rossi, 1999).

Waldorf schools use the concept of looping to its fullest during the grade school years. The class teacher begins this eight-year commitment in grade one and plays a prominent role in shaping the children's grade school experience. He will teach his children the letters of the alphabet and lay the foundation for the development of reading. In the months and years ahead he will introduce his students to cursive writing and punctuation. He will eventually help the children to write their first compositions, teach them the parts of speech, introduce them to expository writing, letter writing, creative writing, poetry, and the critical analysis of literature.

In the beginning of grade one, the class teacher will also introduce arithmetic, showing the children the numbers and teaching them to count by ones, twos, threes, and more. She will demonstrate the four arithmetic processes and help them begin to memorize their times tables and their number facts. In coming years, whole numbers will be divided into fractions, common fractions will be changed into decimal fractions, and decimals will become percents. Eventually these numbers will merge with letters when algebraic terms, equations, and formulae are used. By the end of eighth grade, a similar extensive survey will have been made in the subjects of history, geography, and science as well.

The educational advantages to this approach are myriad. First, it is a most economical use of time. Looping teachers will not spend the first two months of the school year trying to get to know the students. Nor will the students spend the first weeks of the year trying to adjust to new expectations and testing the limits. From an academic perspective, the continuing teacher will already be aware of the individual learning styles—who learns slowly and needs lots of practice, who learns quickly and needs to be challenged. In addition, students' basic strengths and deficiencies will be known, as well as the full extent of the material that was introduced in previous years.

The benefits to this approach occur in other areas as well. Over the past 40 years, families, extended families, and communities have changed dramatically. It is now essential that schools step forward to help provide some of the care and continuity that can no longer be furnished by the neighborhood and the home. Teachers who continue to teach the same children year after year, establish trust that allows the relationship between student and teacher to grow. At the same time, these teachers develop a more discerning eye and are able to perceive problems before they become painfully obvious. The benefits for teachers are equally significant. Vitality replaces complacency, as teachers strive to master a new curriculum each year (Desmon, 2001).

This type of approach asks a great deal of a teacher. The question that is commonly raised with regard to looping is, "What if my child gets the wrong teacher?" The understanding implicit in this question is that if you have a problem with a teacher, the problems will grow exponentially over the years that the teacher and students are together.

The fact is, however, that looping far more often brings out the best in a teacher. Placing teachers in a unique position, where they are called on to commit themselves over a long period of time and to accept the challenge of preparing to teach a new curriculum each year, and by asking teachers to join with parents in accepting extended responsibility for a child's well being, evokes a surprising measure of dedication. At the same time, the commitment to teaching children over an eight-year period attracts individuals who are looking for just such a challenge.

In a *Chicago Sun Times* article by Rosalind Rossi, entitled "Familiar Teachers," she notes, "In [public schools in] the United States, looping is mostly teacher-initiated, and experts say some of the most innovative teachers are asking to loop" (Rossi, 1999). It is not unusual to see successful professionals leave higher paying careers in science, business, law, and the arts to become full-time teachers, excited by the opportunity to make a difference in children's lives. Opportunities such as this ennoble the teaching profession and by so doing attract high-quality candidates to a school.

A great deal is at stake, as there always is in situations that present a special opportunity. The question that arises is: What must be done to safeguard the well being of the children? When looping is in place, the answer rests squarely with the teacher. The same three-dimensional paradigm for students—thinking, feeling, and willing—works in a similar way for teachers. Teachers also need to be *actively* involved in their lessons, thoughtfully aware of the students and the material, and above all *emotionally* involved in their teaching. In short, they need to bring their very best to teaching and then be ready to learn on the job regardless of the number of years that have already been spent in the classroom.

The Journey from Warm to Very Cool

The school day has just ended and the first grade teacher is standing amidst a sea of desks. In a most characteristic way, the first graders' desks have inched forward during the course of the day. This movement of furniture reflects the mood of the students: The first graders want to be as close to their teacher as possible. At lunchtime they vie for the opportunity to sit with their teacher. After lunch, when they are out at recess, they cluster around their teacher, holding his hand and hanging on every word. Out of this deep warmth, affection, and sympathy, the first-grade children simply cannot get enough.

In Waldorf schools, the warm and sympathetic nature of the first grader is reflected in the sweet and caring manner of the first-grade teacher. It is reflected, as well, in the color of the first-grade classroom, usually a warm blend of pink and red. As the children progress through the grades, they move to classrooms that are painted a progression of hues from the colors of the spectrum, from reddish pink to pastel orange, then on to yellow, green and eventually blue and purple in the later years.

If we were to look in on this group of first grade children in their "blue period" six or seven years later, the scene would be very different. The students would now congregate in the back of the room, noticeably distant. And when these adolescent students were asked to take a seat, they would gravitate toward the back rows, rows that are invariably filled first. Instead of leaning forward in anticipation, the seventh graders will want to lean back, tilt their chairs back and turn away from the teacher's gaze. Their response to the teacher is no longer imbued with warmth and sympathy, but is now marked by the cool reserve and distance commonly found in teenagers.

This is the natural emotional progression of childhood, from warmth and connectedness, to coolness, separation, and reserve. Parents experience this shift away from uninhibited closeness when young children no longer sit on their lap or kiss them goodbye in public. This change occurs during the course of the grade school years, and Waldorf teachers accompany parents and children on this developmental journey.

Class teachers are called on to learn many lessons during their eight-year journey, but by far the most surprising lesson that I learned came at the end of my teaching career. It was this lesson that I spoke about at my last class' commencement.

Dear Students,

There is so much that I have learned from you over the years, but by far the most surprising lesson occurred here in this auditorium at the end of last October when you came to school dressed in Halloween costumes. You remember that T. came dressed as Dorothy in her ruby red Doc Martens and with her little rabbit, Toto. That was when I realized what it was like to be your class teacher. It has been an eight-year journey to the Land of Oz.

Back in grade one you were all little munchkins with high voices and I was like the Wizard of Oz. If there were any serious problems, for instance, someone taking your stick while you were out at recess, you would say, "Let's go and ask Mr. Petrash (the all-knowing Oz) what we should do." Back then I could solve all problems. And whenever we had some place to go, you would line right up and we would follow the Yellow Brick Road together. That was how we traveled through the first few grades. We made friends, we sang, and we marched along.

Somewhere around fourth grade that all began to change. We came to the dark part of the forest where the grumpy apple trees grew and there was a different tone in your voice. "Hey, get your hands off that!" and "How would you like it if I did that to you?" And there was no turning back.

Later in sixth grade, the evil winged monkeys appeared, moving through our class, separating friends and dividing us into cliques. In seventh grade, we were heading through the field of poppies and those dreamy flowers were casting their magic spell on you. I would begin main lesson and repeatedly would have to ask you to pick up your head and cover your mouths when you yawned. The only thing that could rouse you from your stupor was snow.

Eventually, in eighth grade we made it to the Emerald City. But now when you came seeking the Wizard, it was all too clear that I was not the all-knowing, all-powerful Oz. Instead I was this little, old guy with a mustache pulling levers and repeating in a loud voice, "Pay no attention to the man behind the curtain!" And you took that advice seriously.

But, if like Dorothy and her friends, you sought brains, courage, heart, and a way home, you have come to the right place. The Waldorf School has tried since its first day to give you the courage the Cowardly Lion sought. With every placemat that you folded after lunch, with every chair that you remembered to push in, every time that you stood up tall to recite your morning verse, and with every main lesson book that you completed to the best of your ability on time, your school has helped you to develop a reservoir of fortitude, and perseverance that is the foundation of courage.

Your school has also tried to give you what the Tin Man longed for—a heart. With every watercolor painting that you made, every song you sang, with every friendship you forged, with every line of every poem you learned by heart, every time a story made you laugh out loud or brought a tear to your eye, your emotional life has grown richer and deeper.

And your school has worked hard to give you the intelligence that the Scarecrow wanted. With every science experiment that you observed with care and wrote down precisely, with every word problem that you solved, every clear and concise sentence that you wrote, and every time you considered an historical event from two or more points of view, you have developed the power of your thinking.

Most of all your school has tried to make you feel at home here on the Earth by recognizing the part of you that is true and unchanging— that spiritual part of you, which your school has always revered. When you live out of what is deepest in you, you will feel at home wherever you go in life. And so students, you can see that it really is as it was in Oz; what you sought was there within you all the time. It was your school's task simply to draw this forth.

References

Desmon, S. (2001, December 9). New grade, same teacher. *The Baltimore Sun*, p. A-1.

Egan, K. (1992). *Imagination in teaching.* Chicago, IL: University of Chicago Press.

Eisner, E. (1998). *The kind of schools we need.* Portsmouth, NH: Heinemann.

Gardner, J. F. (1996). *Education in search of the spirit.* Hudson, NY: Anthroposophic Press.

Healy, J. (1990). *Endangered minds: Why children don't think.* New York: Touchstone.

Murray, D. (1996). *Crafting a life in essay, story, poem.* Portsmouth, NH: Heinemann.

Rossi, R. (1999, October 17). Familiar teachers. *Chicago Sun Times,* A-24.

Smith, B. (1943). *A tree grows in Brooklyn.* New York: Harper Perennial.

Sylwester, R. (1998). Art for the brain's sake. *Educational Leadership* 56 (3), 31-35.

Weinberger, N.M. (1998). The music in our minds. *Educational Leadership* 56 (3), 36-40.

CHAPTER FIVE

The Waldorf High School

"After all, the function of education is to turn out an integrated individual who is capable of dealing with life…"
—J. Krishnamurti

It is a typical high school day, the kind that takes place every spring in hundreds of schools across America. Classes have been over for several hours and the school is remarkably quiet and empty. The only activity inside the building is that which involves the cleaning staff.

Out in the parking lot behind the school, the baseball team is unloading the van, having just returned from an away game. As the coach, I stand with the players as we put away the balls, the bats, and the batting helmets. Our catcher is still unloading his own gear, a large bag that contains his chest protector, shin guards, and mask. He is a senior, and is one of those unique players who evoke a mixture of awe and envy in opposing teams, an all-met player whose homeruns and leadership will eventually lead our team to the Final Four in our state tournament.

As he reaches into the van for his equipment, he begins to sing beautifully and I stop in surprise. He is singing opera and I am immediately struck by the confluence of his talents— his athletic ability and his unique artistic sensibility. I think to myself: "How many coaches in America have a left-handed, power-hitting catcher who lapses into "Don Giovanni" at the end of a long day?"

This experience provided yet another of those moments when I could clearly see the value of a Waldorf education. This young man embodied the results of the three-dimensional approach to education.

Good Habits of Mind

In high school this three-dimensional paradigm continues to be the guiding educational principle. Waldorf high school students are engaged throughout each week actively, emotionally, and thoughtfully, just as they were at other times in their earlier education. However, during this third phase of a young person's education, the emphasis in a Waldorf high school moves decidedly toward thinking, which is developed through the types of subjects that are taught and through the *habits of mind* that are cultivated.

The maturation process that occurs in high school students plays an important role in determining which habits of mind will be cultivated during the four years. According to Douglas Gerwin, the director of the Waldorf High School Training in New Hampshire, each high school year should present a unique question to the students. These underlying questions have an important purpose, to awaken specific aspects of human intelligence.

Ninth-grade students are summoned to exercise powers of exact observation: in the sciences, to describe and draw precisely what happened in the lab experiments and demonstrations; in the humanities, to recount clearly a sequence of events or the nature of a character without getting lost in the confusion of details. The objective here is to train in the student powers of exact observation and reflection so they can experience in the raging storm of phenomena around them the steady ballast of their own thinking... One may summarize the approach of this freshman curriculum with the seminal question: What? What happened? What is going on here? What did you see and hear? (Gerwin, 1997, p. 12).

Gerwin goes on to say that in the tenth grade, observation is expanded to include comparison and the question of "What?" is replaced with "How?" How are acids different from bases? How are men different from women? How do cultural and religious traditions from the Middle East and Far East differ from those in the West?

Eleventh grade develops powers of analysis and abstraction. Gerwin continues:

> The junior year curriculum could be characterized by the theme of invisibility: namely the study of those subjects that draw the student into areas that are not accessible to the experience of our senses... In chemistry, the students enter the invisible kingdom of the atom; in physics they explore the invisible world of electricity (which we can see only in its effects, not in its inherent nature)... These voyages to the invisible landscapes pose a central question intended to strengthen the student's powers of independent analysis and abstract theorizing. The question is "Why? Why are things this way?" (Gerwin, 1997, p.13, 14).

Although the development of thinking is certainly not completed in the high school and will continue in college and in life, the twelfth grade is a time to step back and observe the whole. Synthesis becomes the habit of mind that is trained as the students are asked to broaden their view and see their subjects as part of a whole curriculum. The curriculum poses the questions—"How do I see the world in a non-fragmented way?" "Is there meaning in life?" and finally, "Who am I?" These are presented to the seniors as they look back on their years of study. These questions are raised repeatedly, particularly in the literature study of transcendentalists, with Emerson's "Self Reliance," Whitman's, "Song of Myself," and with Emily Dickinson's poem "The Inner from the Outer."

Keeping these underlying questions in mind, teachers help to develop powers of discernment, enabling students to look closely at the world in which they live and at themselves. The ability to observe, compare, analyze, and synthesize helps young people better understand the world they are inheriting and at the same time, prepares them for finding their place in the world. Because Waldorf education requires inner responsiveness on the part of the students, graduates leave school with a clearer sense of who they are and what they believe to be important, making it possible for them to give direction to their own lives.

In-Depth Study

To develop good habits of mind, schools create learning situations that encourage students to explore subjects deeply, going beyond a superficial understanding. This requires a more intensive focus and in-depth study.

Ted Sizer, the founder of the Coalition for Essential Schools at Brown University, contends that it is not effective to try to cover all the material specified in high school curricula because such attempts to teach all areas of study lead only to a *smorgasbord* of superficial instruction. "My basic conclusion is contained in the aphorism 'Less is more.' I believe that the qualities of mind that should be the goal of high school need time to grow and that they develop best when engaging a few, important ideas, deeply" (Sizer, 1992 p. 89).

Rather than sampling a wide range of diverse material, Waldorf schools choose to delve deeply into selected areas in an effort to provide their students with a more substantive understanding. The main lesson classes that are taught in the high school take place in an hour and forty minute "double" period at the beginning of each school day over the span of three to four weeks. This "block scheduling," which is also a school reform used in mainstream education in both high schools and colleges, is an organizational feature well suited to in-depth study. A dozen subjects are studied in this way over the course of each year. These subjects come from all disciplines ranging from science and math to the humanities and are taught in an intensive, concentrated manner.*

Truth, Beauty, and Goodness

The subjects that a school elects to offer express the values of its institution and or its school system. This is certainly the case in the Waldorf high school, which subscribes to a value-laden approach, one similar in sentiment to what Howard Gardner expresses in his book, *The Disciplined Mind*: "an education for all human beings needs to explore in some depth a set of key human achievements captured in the venerable phrase "the true, the beautiful, and the good" (Gardner, H., 2000, p. 19).

For Rudolf Steiner, the experience of truth, beauty, and goodness was an essential aspect of what children should receive in school. This is also an apt way to describe what Waldorf high school students will encounter through the curriculum. The subjects that are taught can essentially be organized around these ideals.

*At the same time basic instruction in math, English, and foreign language takes place in regularly scheduled classes during the course of each week over the entire school year.)

Truth

High school students actively take up a search for truth. Math and science subjects such as Boolean Algebra, Permutations and Probability, Geology, Optics, or Zoology provide necessary understandings about the tangible world and foster the mental acuity needed for this exploration. But a search for truth is also a personal quest for each individual student. That is why teenagers begin to question adults rather than simply to ask questions. A search for truth inevitably requires that both students and teachers are able to suspend personal beliefs and for an extended period of time entertain other *points of view*. Today, more than ever, issues are rarely so clear as to be one sided. High school teachers must help students develop the habit of considering issues from various points of view.

History teaching in the high school can further this effort by presenting many sides of an issue. With the Civil War, for instance, students can understand both the outrage of the northern abolitionists and the "love of place" that motivated Virginians and especially Robert E. Lee. Students need to experience the worry and danger of the Underground Railroad, as well as the apprehension and pain of the battlefield, the sadness and discouragement of Abraham Lincoln, Daniel Webster, or even Jefferson Davis, and the heartache of the mothers and wives back at home. They should know the desolation and shock of the people of Georgia as Sherman made his "March to the Sea" and they should comprehend as well the disappointment caused by the assassination of Lincoln. Young people must see that even with clear issues, a search for truth is complicated and time consuming, but always worth the effort.

Beauty

The Waldorf curriculum also provides its high school students with the opportunity to consider timeless beauty. In freshman and sophomore year, the study of Art History, a two-part survey course, enables the students to experience, know, and recreate works of lasting artistic value. The eleventh-grade study of the History of Music offers the same opportunity, as does the senior-year study of the History of Architecture. All of these courses underscore the importance of beauty and place it in the context of human history.

Goodness

High school students also need an experience of the good. The National Association of Secondary School Principals (NASSP) states in its report, *Breaking Ranks: Changing an American Institution,* "that schools must unabashedly teach students about key virtues… Some educators may feel uncomfortable about accepting this assignment, but we believe certain enduring virtues are universal to principled Americans. In an era when children are killing children and children are giving birth to children, high schools cannot afford to shirk this duty" (NASSP, 1996a, p. 30).

Value-laden instruction is a complicated matter fraught with a wide array of difficulties, but one that cannot be avoided. Although it is often fruitless to provide direct instruction about virtue, examples of individuals from history and literature who have wrestled with moral questions enable students to explore and define their own beliefs. In high school, the main lesson in Dante's *Inferno* brings students face to face with the conflict of Good and Evil. In the study of the epic tale, *Parsifal,* the role of personal moral responsibility is explored. And in the reading of Victor Hugo's classic novel, *Les Miserables,* the possibility of human transformation is viewed through the character of Jean Valjean. Other books such as the *Upanishads* or the *Bhagavad Gita* are used in a Waldorf high school because they raise serious ethical questions, ones that encourage students to consider goodness as an ideal that is as worthy of our attention as truth and beauty.

The Pedagogy at Work

In a freshman class at Oberlin College in Ohio, students are receiving an unexpected and rather surprising assignment. The professor tells them that he is going to collect their notes at the start of the next day's class. After a flurry of gasps and groans, one student asks, "Which notes?"

"Your class notes," the professor replies.

"But which class notes?" the student responds, "The ones I take each day or the ones that I rewrite at night?"

Now it is the professor who is surprised. "Who told you that I was going to collect your notes?"

"No one," the student rejoins, "this is the way I was taught to take notes."

"Where did you go to school?" the professor asks skeptically.

The student answers, "A small school on Long Island, the Waldorf School."

"Oh, that explains it," the professor replies, satisfied at last.

The value of the Waldorf educational philosophy should be evident in its ability to put educational principles into practice. One way to assess if this is indeed being done effectively would be to examine the Waldorf program in the light of commonly accepted educational criteria.

The late Ernest Boyer, former Commissioner of Education, Chancellor of the State University of New York, and president of the Carnegie Foundation for the Advancement of Teaching, took part in an extensive study of secondary education in America and proposed that high schools should strive to meet four essential goals.

> First, the high school should help all students develop the capacity to think critically and communicate effectively through a mastery of language.

> Second, the high school should help all students learn about themselves, the human heritage, and the interdependent world in which they live through a core curriculum based upon consequential human experiences common to all people.

Third, the high school should prepare all students for work and further education through a program of electives that develop individual aptitudes and interests.

Fourth, the high school should help all students fulfill their social and civic obligations through school and community service (Boyer, 1983, p. 66, 67).*

These four goals provide a viable way to measure the soundness of the Waldorf approach to high school education.

Communicating Clear Thinking through the Mastery of Language

With regard to the first of Boyer's goals, the section of this chapter that discusses good habits of mind (pages 84-87) shows that Waldorf high schools offer a comprehensive approach to the development of critical thinking. What has not been stated explicitly, however, is the role that the mastery of written and spoken language plays in that process.

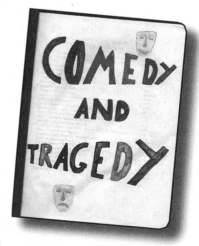

Each high school student writes, on the average, three compositions each week. These pieces vary in type from experiment observations, to informative descriptions, to narrative accounts, essays, research projects, and literary interpretations. Almost all of these compositions will become the text of the student's main lesson books, accounts of the material studied in each of the dozen or so main lesson blocks in the year. These books contain the essential information from the lessons and serve as a textbook to the students.

*Reprinted with permission by The Carnegie Foundation for the Advancement of Teaching.

In addition to providing continuous opportunities for writing, the extended main lesson format encourages classroom discourse, requiring students to express their ideas orally through the regular review of the previous day's work and through discussion of new material. In each instance, the school supports the students in the delicate process of ascertaining and giving voice to their own thoughts.

Understanding Our Human Heritage

With regards to the second of the Carnegie Foundation's goals, it is clear that Waldorf schools' approach is decidedly "humanistic." An understanding of "human heritage" is placed at the forefront of the Waldorf program. Ancient cultures from Asia, Africa, and the Americas, from Buddha and Lao Tzu to the Bushmen of the Kalihari and the Native Sioux , are all considered from the point of view of their wisdom, faith, and insight. At the same time, our modern civilization and its current and sometimes tragic events are also examined at length. In this way the Waldorf high school is able to blend two essential considerations noted by Howard Gardner in his recent book, *The Disciplined Mind*: "We need an education that is deeply rooted in two apparently contrasting but actually complementary considerations: what is known about the human condition in its timeless aspects; and what is known about the pressures and challenges, and opportunities of the contemporary scene" (Gardner, 2000 p. 20).

Preparing Students for the Future—Elective Courses

As a young graduate student in education, I visited a local Waldorf school and saw a display of work from high school students. I remember pausing in front of a table and staring at a red flannel shirt that one of the senior boys had sewn, and a beautifully drawn skeleton of a horse in his biology main lesson book, and then at a large exquisite stained glass project and a beautiful piece of calligraphy. I had a bachelor's degree and was on the verge of completing my masters, but I lacked the abilities that this high school student had. I knew it and I felt shortchanged. But I also knew immediately that this was the type of school in which I wanted to teach.

Because the three-dimensional paradigm matters as much in the high school as it does in the preschool and grade school, all students take a combination of classes that require manual skill and artistic ability, as well as academic understanding. Courses such as choral singing, stone sculpture, and eurhythmy (a form of movement set to music or speech that was developed by Rudolf Steiner and taught at most Waldorf schools) are required courses for all students because they are essential in developing well-rounded individuals.

Within a framework of a balanced education students are encouraged to choose electives, which can range from the highly technical subjects (robotics) to the most basic (blacksmithing), and from the 21st century with computer graphics and web design to madrigal singing, 18th century chamber music, or an in-depth consideration of the Civil Rights Movement or Darwin's *Origin of the Species*. These choices are not necessarily career track electives, but they do allow students to follow their interests, deepen their understanding, and perfect their skills.

Social and Civic Responsibility

Anyone who spends time with American high school students cannot help but notice a striking degree of self-centeredness. Teenagers are, by nature, self-conscious and self-involved. When affluence is added to the mix, it exacerbates the situation further. For that reason, Waldorf schools, like so many other schools across the country, have institutionalized service programs to help young people acquire social awareness and demonstrate social responsibility.

Service-based construction programs like *Habitat for Humanity* or *Christmas in April* are often popular with Waldorf schools because they provide hands-on, concrete ways to help. With supervision and materials provided by local construction companies, high school students are able to spend weekend time making repairs and painting the homes of the elderly, the disabled, and the less-fortunate.

Another opportunity for social service is found at local soup kitchens. Waldorf high school students often perform their service as a class, going to a local shelter together to prepare and serve lunch several times during the school year. This arrangement provides an important opportunity, enabling the students to transform their idealism and concern into action—in short, to think globally but act locally.

Working locally is equally important when it comes to environmental issues. Waldorf students need to be aware of environmental issues in their school, not just in the rain forest.

Student government should be involved in school decisions on paper use, nutritional and packaging issues concerning lunch, and the recycling of cardboard, plastic, and aluminum. These small decisions are important because they help Waldorf students experience the conflict between our ideals and our own personal convenience.

Small Is Beautiful

Waldorf high schools do more than an adequate job of meeting the educational goals set forth by the Carnegie Foundation in its study of American high schools. And yet, concerns are not uncommon.

Perhaps the most common criticism directed at Waldorf high schools has centered on size. Parents, students, and even teachers have at times felt that the schools are too small. Typical enrollments of approximately 100 students change social interactions in a variety of ways, including the dramatic experience of school spirit prevalent at large high school sporting events, and the traditional *high school scene* with large cafeterias, well-equipped gymnasiums, and large groups of students.

Smaller budgets mean fewer faculty members, and students miss the possibility of having new teachers year after year. Housed on the same campus and often in the same building as the preschool and the grade school, Waldorf students often complain about the familiarity of being in the same place and with the same students and teachers for 12 to 14 years. The perception is that small is a disadvantage, but according to a recent study of American high schools by the National Association of Secondary School Principals, this is not the case.

> During much of this century, reformers sought to shut small high schools and herd youngsters into ever larger schools

that styled themselves after the factory model. Experts perceived bigness as a *sine qua non* of excellence. This paradigm, with its vast array of offerings, represented the epitome of educational progress. But students are not pieces on an assembly line and knowledge is not an inert commodity to pour into vessels like soft drink syrup in a bottling plant. The impersonal nature of high school leaves too many youngsters alienated from the learning process (NASSP, 1996b, p. 11).

Clearly, the "weakness" of a Waldorf high school is also its strength. The familiarity that makes young people feel uncomfortable also makes them members of a community. It insures that they are known and cared for and that changes in their behavior and appearance do not go unnoticed.

This insightful passage by Theodore Sizer from his book, *Horace's Compromise: The Dilemma of the American High School*, clearly shows the anonymity that students seek.

> Her name was Melissa. She entered the classroom alone…Looking at no one in particular. Melissa headed toward a desk to the teacher's left, against a wall…She said nothing to her neighbors, but seemed at ease with them and they with her. She looked about her, neither pleasantly nor unpleasantly, with no particular recognition, enthusiasm, curiosity, or hostility…
>
> Melissa watched all…without animation. Her face was not blank, quite; there was ennui, acceptance, a trace or wariness. A question was directed to her. She looked at the teacher with little change in expression. A pause. I don't understand. (The teacher) repeated the question, kindly, without reproach. Another pause. I don't know… Melissa speaking slowly said something, a phrase using words earlier spoken during the teacher's lecture. It was enough to end the exchange, but not enough to provoke a counterquestion or a follow up by the teacher.
>
> Melissa, however unwittingly, was a master of non-

engagement. She sat at the side. She didn't move much, thus drawing attention to herself. She did not offer ideas to the class, and when questioned answered with something just plausible and relevant enough to avoid being chided for inattention…She was an educational artful dodger with considerable skill… I could imagine Melissa moving through her entire school day in (this) fashion (Sizer, 1984, p. 161, 162).*

This non-engagement is a challenge to teachers. Many students in high schools across the country slip by disengaged with only a modicum of effort, and no one notices. In contrast, Waldorf high schools discourage anonymity. When a teacher instructs approximately 100 different students each year as opposed to 300, she is able to notice the quiet, disengaged student and intervene. Students cannot avoid responsiveness when they sit in smaller classes, face to face with an attentive teacher who has known them and possibly their siblings for an extended period of time. More so, when a team of high school teachers with many eyes and a variety of perspectives meets regularly to discuss the students as Waldorf teachers do each week, the students' needs become more clear to everyone. This underscores the notion that *the whole is greater than the sum of its parts.*

Schools need to meet the boys and girls such as Melissa who reside on the periphery, but they also need to confront the students who are overly assertive and aggressive. Every high school has its bullies, both girls and boys. Some are physical, some verbal, and some practice emotional intimidation. These students can prove just as elusive as quiet students because they hide behind their peers and behind a persona of potential defiance. In large schools the crowd obscures these students, but in small schools they are painfully obvious.

*Reprinted by permission of Houghton Mifflin Company.

Balanced Development in the High School

In either case, the teachers hold the key to the students' ability to change through direct contact with these students. It takes a great deal of effort on the part of the teacher to intervene successfully to effect change. In a Waldorf high school, however, the three-dimensional paradigm supports that effort.

The non-engaged student and the overly assertive are lacking balanced development. The non-engaged student lacks involvement, that volitional aspect that is cultivated in a Waldorf school from the earliest years. Active involvement, or *will development*, is the basis of the preschool program as well as a key component of the grade school. It must continue to be fostered in the high school as well through movement and artistic work, classroom participation, and extracurricular activities.

In the Waldorf high school program, where sports teams and dramatic productions accept all students rather than offering tryouts, the opportunity for activity and involvement increases. Perceptive teachers can see the long-distance runner in the solitary student or exceptional basketball ability in the seemingly unathletic, quiet girl who can apply her unwavering focus, dedication, and intelligence to a one-on-one defense. When these students are encouraged and supported to explore new abilities in unfamiliar situations, they grow in confidence. But, most of all, these active experiences strike at the root of non-engagement. However, these changes cannot happen without an advocate. That is why many Waldorf high schools provide a personal advisor for each high school student.

In a similar way, the aggressive student is lacking in balanced development. In this instance it is the emotional aspect that is undeveloped. With bullies, sensitivity, consideration, and compassion, are all strikingly absent. These students form critical judgments about their classmates and teachers and often manifest these negative judgments in unfortunate actions, actions that can be heartless and cruel. It is emotional engagement that is missing or distorted in what they do. And this is precisely what needs to be encouraged in high school. It is not uncommon that artistic ability sleeps within the aggressive student. Musical ability, dramatic ability, and visual artistic talent often reside in the most challenging and aggressive students.

> *"I shall create. If not a note, a hole. If not an overture, a desecration."*
> —Gwendolyn Brookes (speaking about an angry adolescent) (Brookes, 1987)

When high school programs require all students to be artistically engaged it is easier for difficult students to find an artistic outlet for their frustrations. These students often have latent talents that have gone unnoticed. When an advisor can look closely and with sufficient insight to recognize the musical or dramatic ability that has gone undeveloped in a difficult student, it can clear the way for healing and positive change.

This is not just a *Waldorf* understanding. Educators nationwide have recognized the arts as an invaluable tool for helping young people find direction in their lives. Author Bill Shore points this out in his recent book, *The Cathedral Within: Transforming Your Life by Giving Something Back.*

> The Chicago Children's Choir (is) the largest choral and performance training group of its kind in the United States. As much as (its director) Nancy Carstedt loves music, that is not the focal point of her work. Her work is about saving children's lives. She succeeds at it by letting kids into a world they've never imagined, exposing them to discipline and commitment and excellence ... and by doing whatever is necessary to enable them to create and experience excellence themselves...The choir is multiracial,

multicultural, and like any choir, harmony is its business (Shore, 1999, p. 79).

On the other hand, when high school programs ignore arts education, the results can be disastrous. This was underscored by the late music educator, Charles Fowler. "My observations in schools are that drugs, crime, indifference and insensitivity tend to run rampant in schools that deprive students of instruction in the arts" (Fowler, 1996, p. 12, 13).

Restoring Balance

When Waldorf teachers work with challenging students, they proceed on two levels: They deal with problematic behavior and then they invariably turn to the root cause of the problem. Almost always, the difficulties that are uncovered indicate a one-sided and incomplete development of the three essential capacities—thinking, feeling, and willing—that are at the heart of Waldorf education. This incomplete development occurs for a variety of reasons—mis-education, difficulties in the home, or a physiological problem—but in any case it requires a high school teacher's unwavering dedication to restore balance through teaching.

This is the same educational ideal that not only shapes the work of the high school, but of all three phases of a Waldorf education—preschool, grade school, and high school. The fundamental understanding is that a student's healthy development must be fostered by an education that is *heartfelt* and hands-on as well as academic. It is only through a well-balanced approach to teaching that we can help students realize all that they can do and help them to become adults who can realize their full human potential.

References

Boyer, E. (1983). *High school: A report on secondary education in America.* New York: Harper & Row.

Brookes, G. (1987). *Blacks.* Chicago: Third World Press.

Fowler, C. (1996). *Strong arts, strong schools: The promising potential and shortsighted disregard of the arts in American schools.* New York: Oxford University Press.

Gardner, H. (2000). *The disciplined mind: Beyond facts and standardized tests.* New York: Penguin Books.

Gerwin, D. & L. Harris. (1997). *Genesis of a Waldorf high school: A source book.* Wilton, NH: High Mowing School.

Krishnamurti, J. (2000). Educating the educator. *Parabola*, 25 (3), 85-89.

National Association of Secondary School Principals. (1996a). *Breaking new ranks: Changing an American institution*. Reston, VA: Author.

National Association of Secondary School Principals. (1996b). *Breaking new ranks: Changing an American institution: An executive summary.* Reston, VA: Author.

Shore, B. (1999). *The cathedral within: Transforming your life by giving something back.* New York: Random House.

Sizer, T. (1984). *Horace's compromise: The dilemma of the American high school.* New York: Houghton Mifflin.

CHAPTER SIX

The Essential Parent

"What is asked of us as parents is sometimes more than we would expect of any person. That is as it should be; for as parents we have been given the wonderful challenge of growing as human beings while at the same time giving the highest service possible."
—Franklin Kane, Parents as People

It is a weekday evening and the classroom is filled with prospective parents. They have come to the school for one of the monthly information evenings to find out more about the Waldorf School and to see if this might be the right place for their child. An introductory talk about the school, detailing the fundamental aspects of the program, has just ended and now the questions come. As is almost always the case, someone asks: "How do students do when they leave your school?"

This question presents an opening to speak about the school's successes, about the students who have gone to Yale and Stanford, about the scholarship winners, the athlete-scholars, the musicians, and successful business people. But before the school takes all of the credit, I always add that it has been my experience that the students who do the best are the ones whose families have provided them with educational direction and clear expectations. These are usually the students who have eaten dinner with their parents, who have been at home on school nights, who have come to know that homework is a top priority, ahead of shopping at the mall, going to a sporting event, or talking on the telephone. These students have the understanding that schooling is their work and if they are to succeed, they must give their best effort.

My 25 years of experience as a teacher has shown me conclusively that parents are an essential part of the educational equation. The relationship between the parent and the child, or for that matter, between the parent and the teacher, is significant. Simply stated, when parents invest time and energy in furthering their child's education, good things happen.

The question, "What can we do at home to support our child's education?" is an important consideration for parents of young children, but important as well right on through high school and into college. Perhaps the best starting point for parents is the same three-dimensional paradigm that is central to Waldorf education. If parents are able to engage their children actively, emotionally, and thoughtfully at home, they will be fostering the same healthy development.

Actively Engaged at Home

One way that parents can support children's Waldorf education is to be sure that they are actively engaged at home. One of the more noticeable changes in children's lives outside of school in the last 50 years is the dramatic decrease in activity. In the past, children walked home from school and ran right out to play. Once outdoors they rode bikes, put on roller skates, played tag and "kick the can," or simply skipped; they played catch or house, or just walked and talked. They had companions and they were active.

Today, children travel by school bus. They often come home to an empty house, fix themselves something to eat, then head for the couch with a newspaper, a magazine, the television remote, or video game controls. After sitting all day in school, they sit some more. It is no wonder that obesity is a growing problem for today's youth.

Aside from the occasional scrapes and bruises, active children are healthy children. Parents who are willing to extend themselves in an effort to encourage activity can further healthy development. The same balance between outdoor activity and indoor activity can be an objective for the family, as well. If parents can help young children become accustomed at an early age to playing outside for some amount of time each day, then the vigorous play that children need and often long for will become part of their routine outside of school.

Unfortunately, for children today, it is often no longer safe to play outside unsupervised. For this reason, working parents who want to see that their children are spending time outside will have to use the weekend and holidays to further their efforts. Regular activity, even if it is once or twice a week, will still serve to make children more robust and vigorous. Whether it is bicycle riding or hiking, ice skating or raking leaves, children who become accustomed to being active out of doors develop a vitality that enhances their attentiveness and responsiveness. This, in turn, improves their school performance.

Children can be active indoors as well, and they benefit from helping around the home. Regular chores at home enhance children's development. Clearing the table or cleaning the bathroom has a sequence and a format. In developing these habits, children learn valuable skills, including how to organize their efforts by dividing large jobs into manageable parts. They also learn to pay attention to details, to persevere, and to be part of a team. As children become accustomed to working on a regular basis, their capacity for work grows and they become able to handle large tasks in any context and not be overwhelmed. When parents can see that the skills that children gain from these efforts are transferable, they can have confidence that every task that their child does well at home helps them to do well at school. And every task that children learn to do day in and day out, whether it is making their bed or washing the dishes, develops perseverance and determination.

Although a noticeable lethargy appears in the teenage years when young people often choose to "do nothing" or simply "hang out," there still is a latent desire to be active. Anyone associated with wilderness programs and sports teams notices how much more alive and animated young people become after physical exertion. Parents serve their adolescents and teenagers well when they discreetly and effectively encourage physical activity.

For most parents, sports teams provide the vehicle for strenuous exercise, and it is true that in the right situation, being on a team can develop admirable qualities in addition to physical resilience and stamina. Teamwork, perseverance, and learning to think on one's feet are all valuable character traits, and yet, being on a sports team, in and of itself, is no guarantee that healthy development will be furthered. Parents who encourage a variety of activities and a variety of sports, as opposed to specialization, broaden both their children's interests and their athletic ability.

Sometimes the right activity for a child is neither convenient nor cheap. One of the girls that I taught loved to play hockey. She was a defense(wo)man who handled a hockey stick as well as she played violin, and skated as well as she wrote. When she came off the ice, her cheeks were red and her eyes were bright; she just loved the irony of being a quiet girl who was able to play this physically intimidating game. Her parents were not big hockey fans, nor did they enjoy the practices at late hours or the long travel distances for away games. They simply supported their daughter's interest and believed that her participation would make her a more complete person.

A wide variety of activities are favorites with teenagers. Mountain biking, rock climbing, and kayaking are popular because they challenge young people to do what seems impossible. Succeeding in challenging situations builds self-esteem and quiet confidence and yet there are other less perilous ways to accomplish this. Sometimes hard work provides the confidence young people seek.

"A number of years ago the State of California offered a work program for young people similar to the Civilian Conservation Corps, the federally funded program during the Depression. The California program advertised itself as offering hard work, low pay, and long hours. It had a waiting list" (Petrash, 2000, p. 26). Strenuous physical labor develops confidence, as well.

It is also easy for young people to develop self-esteem through the mastery of skills. When teenagers have a skill that they can do as well as an adult, their confidence grows. The students I know have been interested in a number of areas, including carpentry, bicycle repair, emergency medical treatment, and animal husbandry. Having these capabilities develops teenagers' feelings of self-worth and allows them to work side by side with adults. This gives them the rite of passage into adult society that they seek and is often missing in today's society. Although the desire to be active is most pronounced in the young child, it is clearly important right through the teenage years.

Having stated this, I would be remiss if I did not mention something about the paradoxical nature of parenting. Structured activity is important at home, but too much structure is detrimental. We also need free time. More and more children are completely booked seven days a week. They hustle from school to music lessons to ballet, from the orthodontist to horseback riding to soccer, with little or no time to catch their breath. Children need down time, time to relax, time to be a little bored, time to exhale.

Emotionally Engaged at Home

Children's emotional development begins long before they ever enter school. During the first years of childhood, the interactions that parents have with their children affect this development. When we hold our children, speak to them, sing to them, walk with them, and reprimand them, we help to establish their emotional response to the world. The sound of our voice and the pressure of our hand will foster a connection or disconnection with the world by letting children know if the world is scary or safe.

Helping children to feel secure in the world is important work for parents. Something as simple as establishing a daily routine with regular times for meals and for naps can reassure children and help them see that the world makes sense because of its predictability. Special events like story time or a song and prayer at bedtime become predictable times when a child can anticipate and count on positive and caring human contact. Such times add emotional stability to a child's life.

Healthy emotional development cannot take place without interactions with other people. Unfortunately, children today spend too much time in isolation. They play inside more than outside, and their contact with other children is often limited to organized get-togethers, classes, and teams. When they are at home, children often isolate themselves behind headphones and closed doors. With telephones, televisions, and CD players in their bedrooms, children today find it easy to retreat into solitude. Parents need to encourage children to interact with others. The unfortunate fact is that children now have approximately one-third fewer face-to-face encounters than they did 40 years ago (Cordes and Miller, 2000).

A common place for face-to-face encounters to occur is the dinner table. It is there that children learn to speak with others, to express themselves clearly and in complete sentences, and most importantly, to listen. Teachers bemoan the deterioration of listening skills among children. This is one important place where parents can help to counteract that problem. For many families, dinnertime together has become an endangered activity, especially as children grow older and schedules become increasingly complex.

Another important way children can be emotionally engaged is through artistic expression. When parents want to foster emotional development, they can do this by giving their children opportunities to draw or sing or play a musical instrument at home. These undertakings enable children to find non-verbal ways to express what they are not always able to put into words.

Although music, dance, and drawing lessons often start at an earlier age, it is around adolescence, when most children are inclined to stop, that their value grows immeasurably. Often during the tumultuous teenage years, young people will turn to their music, poetry, or drawing as a refuge, a safe haven where they can begin to understand and express the strong feelings that are surging within them. At all ages children need their parents to support their emotional well being.

Helping Children Think for Themselves

The child's three capacities for thinking, feeling, and doing are interrelated. What parents do with children will help to form an emotional bond with them, and the feelings of security and happiness that parents are able to engender will help children to be receptive to the world and to learn from their experiences. In her book, *Endangered Minds*, Jane Healy writes, "Children who have been talked to, and read to, are at a real advantage. They've learned how to listen and how to pay attention" (Healy, 1990 p. 80). In a recent article in U.S. News and World Report (October 30th, 2000), Dr. Stanley Greenspan expressed a similar sentiment when he stated, "A warm loving relationship is very important for intellectual development. Children form their capacity to think and self-image based on their back and forth interactions."

Parents nurture their children's intelligence when they spend quality time with their children from an early age, interacting with them in a thoughtful manner, engaging them in conversation, and giving them their undivided attention.

Another way to assist the development of thinking is by exposing children to new experiences so that their understanding and interest in the world grows. Helping children expand their horizons with books, trips to museums, and experiences in nature is part of a parent's job description.

Parents who are able to help their teenage children broaden their interests are doing important work. Adolescents are markedly conventional and, for many, doing something out of the ordinary is unappealing. Videos, movies, and rock concerts all rank high on the list of preferred activities. But the surprising enjoyment derived from going to a play or taking an extended bicycle tour has left such an indelible and favorable impression on so many young people that parents should try to foster these experiences as well.

As children get older, they become more reluctant to show interest in obvious ways. Finding out what older children's interests are can be a covert operation in which parents need to be attentive to any sign, learning to detect the slightest hint of enthusiasm or sympathy. Tact can be the most important factor, as any outward sign of interest from a parent can prove disastrous and thwart any possibility of participation. Parenting is a dance and good dancers are able to affect their partner's movement in the gentlest ways without making it obvious that they are leading. It is in this way that parents can help their older children develop and pursue their interests.

Parents can also help develop their older children's capacity to think by engaging them in substantive conversations about current cultural, political, or sporting events. Young people have so many opinions, especially about controversial issues, and we should elicit them and show interest in what they have to say. We should seek their opinions on a variety of topics and listen carefully. Teenagers should be encouraged to express their thoughts clearly and parents should help them pursue their thoughts on ever-deeper levels. But most of all, parents, like teachers, need to respect a young person's ability to think independently, knowing that this is a work in progress. Young people may sometimes seem to change their opinions as often as their clothes, but this is a positive sign that shows the ability to think for oneself is becoming more pronounced.

The Challenge of Homework

Waldorf parents invest a great deal in their child's education—time, effort, and often a considerable amount of money—and protecting this investment requires continuous involvement in a number of different ways. A parent's responsibility will concern more than just helping with homework.

In fact, Waldorf schools tend to give less homework than other independent schools. Homework assignments start gradually in the elementary school and often no homework is given in grades one or two. In grade three, when it is customary for homework to begin, assignments are usually only 10 to 15 minutes long and only given every other day.

A small amount of homework in the early grades is sufficient to help children develop the habit of taking out-of-school assignments seriously and doing them in a timely and responsible manner. It is important that parents help children find a consistent time and place for doing homework in order to establish a regular routine. When homework is done carefully on a regular basis, good habits are formed and these habits strengthen children and gradually enable them to manage the larger assignments that will be given in the upper grades.

Even in the Waldorf upper-grade classrooms, homework assignments are rarely so extensive that they preclude the possibility of students having time outside of school to be both active and creative. The implicit understanding is that all students should have the time each day for physical and artistic activity, as well as homework. By the time a student is in high school, he or she will need to practice a musical instrument about an hour each day. If you add to the music practice participation on a sports team, which is also an important activity for teenage girls and boys, then a student does not need to have more than one to two hours of homework.

Because each of the three capacities—thinking, feeling, and willing—is valuable, their development in the home is also worth safeguarding. It stands to reason that parents who value a well-rounded approach to education will see the value in shorter homework assignments, because there is still time for basketball or soccer, for drawing, dance, or a musical instrument, for a face-to-face conversation, and of course, time to help out around the home by clearing the table and doing the dishes. When lengthy homework assignments keep students from having this time, they undermine rather than enhance a young person's development.

Empowering Parents

When parents understand and embrace the principles of child development that are at the heart of a Waldorf education, they can make choices at home that support the work that is being done at school. The goal with parent education at every level of a Waldorf school should be empowerment.

Parents are faced with myriad choices each week. Some are relatively benign, such as whether or not to serve dessert or arrange a play date. Other decisions, however, impact more directly on the child's education, like the amount of television viewing or computer use that is allowed. When parents are able to consider these "activities" from the vantage point of the three-dimensional understanding, certain questions come into focus immediately. For instance, regarding television, parents can ask themselves, "How is a child's active nature engaged through television viewing or, for that matter, through computer use?" For young children particularly, watching television encourages passivity, leaving them mesmerized and listless. A second question that arises is, "What kind of emotional development does television viewing foster?" Does it foster sensitivity and security? Or does it give rise to premature sexual interest, sassiness, or fear (knowing that one of the goals of advertising is to trigger our *flight or fight response* in order to heighten our attention and make a more lasting impression). And with regard to the development of intelligence, how does television affect language development and attention span, not to mention a willingness to read extensively? It is part of schools' work to provide information to help parents make sound parenting decisions, with the understanding that, in the end, what takes place in the home is the responsibility of the parents.

Investing time and effort in parent education is one of the best decisions any school can make. When parents and teachers form a team, working in accord to meet the needs of children, significant educational progress can be made. Parents are such an important part of the educational process that their involvement and commitment cannot be underestimated. Their active, supportive presence adds solidity to the school and stability to their child's educational journey.

References

Cordes, C. & E. Miller. (2000, September 12). *Fool's gold: A critical look at computers in the classroom.* College Park, MD: Alliance for Childhood.

Healy, J. (1990). *Endangered minds: Why children don't think.* New York: Touchstone.

Kelly, K. (2000, October 30). Child docs to parents: Stay home and save your kids. *U.S. News and World Report.*

Petrash, J. (2000). *Covering home: Lessons on the art of fathering from the game of baseball.* Beltsville, MD: Robins Lane Press.

CHAPTER SEVEN

A Teacher's Journey

"Many programs are trying to effect educational reform
from the outside in, but the greatest immediate power we
have is to work to reform from the inside out. Ultimately,
human wholeness does not come from changes in our
institutions, it comes from the reformation of our hearts."
—Parker Palmer, *The Courage to Teach*

I had the opportunity to work with a group of teachers in a
public school in Baltimore, Maryland. This was not a "model"
school, one where visitors are brought to see the successes of
the system. This was an *at-risk* school that had been
reconstituted by the city because test scores had fallen. Yet, I
found my visits to this school reassuring. The children were
great, the principal was open and innovative, and the teachers,
who were dedicated professionals, surprised me time and again.

When I first sat with the teachers, I asked them what kind of
students they were in elementary school. I wanted to encourage
them to think like children, to remember what it was like to
fidget, to daydream, and to watch the clock. I succeeded in
getting them to recall their school days, but their responses took
me by surprise. Almost exclusively, their memories turned out to
be the recollections of children who loved their teachers—

children who loved school and who played school at home. These were individuals whose own teachers had inspired and excited them. These were the children of teachers, the children of principals, and students of teachers who had conveyed an infectious enthusiasm for the profession. These were men and women who entered the teaching profession with idealism and, from the start, believed that being a teacher was a dignified undertaking, a vocation where a person could make a difference.

So many educators begin their professional journeys with similar idealism and hope. Not all survive. Cold cynicism seeps into the profession through bureaucratic cracks, through the weight of demeaning paperwork, through the pressures of testing, and through a multitude of compromises with political and business interests. This cynicism dampens and often extinguishes the enthusiasm and commitment of those who are not deeply impassioned.

Good teachers learn early to protect themselves. They close their classroom doors, dedicate themselves to their ideals in private, and befriend other dedicated teachers. Most of all, they turn to the children and thrive on the immediacy of that relationship. They take solace in the knowledge that their work is as important for the children as it is for them. With that understanding, they commit themselves repeatedly to being good teachers.

What Makes a Good Teacher?

In his book, *The Courage to Teach,* Parker Palmer writes:

> Good teaching cannot be reduced to technique; good teaching comes from the identity and integrity of the teacher...My evidence for this claim comes, in part, from years of asking students to tell me about their good

teachers. Listening to those stories, it becomes impossible to claim that all good teachers use similar techniques. Some lecture non-stop and others speak very little; some stay close to their material and others loose the imagination. Some teach with the carrot and others with the stick.

But in every story I have heard, good teachers share one trait: a strong sense of personal identity infuses their work. 'Dr. A is really there when she teaches,' a student tells me, or 'Mr. B has such enthusiasm for his subject,' or 'You can tell that this is really Prof. C's life' (Palmer, 1998, p. 10, 11).*

The heart and soul of an effective teacher are noticeably present in the classroom and the same three-dimensional paradigm can easily be observed. Good teachers give themselves to their work the same way that children give themselves to theirs—actively, emotionally, and thoughtfully.

The Active Teacher

When I first started out as a teacher, I worked in a New York City Public School with a dedicated young faculty. Each Friday after school let out, some of us would gather at a local tavern, drink a beer, and talk about our work. These were the only faculty meetings we had. Difficult children were discussed, school programs were developed, and a community of teachers was formed as we shared experiences, successes, and of course, our disappointments. Our teaching was never seen as a nine-to-three job. It was always understood, even by new teachers, that what we did after the children went home would determine tomorrow's success.

*This material is used by permission of Jossey-Bass, Inc., a subsidiary of John Wiley & Sons, Inc.

When I was a graduate student studying to become a Waldorf teacher, this aspect of a teacher's responsibility was absolutely clear. One of my professors expressed it succinctly. "Most people work nine to five [at least back then] and you work nine to three, so you need to prepare from three to five."

Two hours of preparation each day became my benchmark. When school ended, I knew that I still had a couple of hours of work to do. I could do it at home, later in the day, or I could do it right then and there in the classroom. The choice was mine.

Sometimes the work was physical—straightening the rows, cleaning a closet, dusting a counter, pulling the dead leaves off of plants, or changing a bulletin board. Sometimes the work was more technical—marking math papers, editing compositions, or researching the next day's lesson. And sometimes the work was reflective—thinking about a difficult child, assessing a failed lesson, seeking for ways to make my teaching more alive.

At times my preparation work flowed immediately from one area to another. This could happen when I was moving a desk only to have its contents cascade onto the floor, revealing the mysterious inner sanctum. As I would pick up the contents of the desk, I would glimpse a unique view of a particular child's world and I would realize how much there was still to know about my students.

It was by working like this each day after school and on the weekend that I forged a bond with my work. Teaching was more than just a job and a paycheck. This was my calling; this was work I could put my heart into.

There were a number of small, unusual things that I loved about being a Waldorf teacher. One was that the teachers were given keys to the school. As a former New York City public school teacher, I knew what a luxury it was to be able to enter a school building at any time and work in my classroom. Taking advantage of this opportunity, I often made my way over to school late on Sunday afternoons. Invariably, there were a few other cars in the parking lot. Like ballplayers who arrive at the park early for extra batting practice, these were the teachers who shared a love of the game. I'd always stop to say hello, but not to chat for long. We were there on business. I simply wanted to greet them and to acknowledge how much I loved working with other teachers who worked hard.

The Emotionally Active Teacher

Good teachers come to school early or they stay late. They teach when they're ill rather than call a substitute, and they'll do school work even when they're off. They sometimes dream about their students and they like to *talk shop*. In short, good teachers care.

Good teachers care about the students and stand by them during difficult times. Good teachers love their children. Yet, early in my career, I wondered exactly what that meant. I felt that this was something I should do, but didn't know exactly how. There are always children who delight us, who are kindred spirits. But what about the more challenging children? How are we to be sure that we love them? Then, one day I got the answer.

I had to arrange a parent conference for a difficult child. In the meeting I was describing the child's difficulties to his mother in an extended fashion. The child was disruptive in class, his work was sloppy, his assignments were often incomplete, and he turned in his homework sporadically.

"Yes, I know," the mother said, discouraged. Then suddenly she brightened and added with a smile, "But isn't he a lively boy?" This was the perfect example of a parent's love.

In listening to parents, and especially to mothers, in meetings and in conversations, I have noticed that this is something that loving parents will invariably do. They continually see the best in the child. As a teacher I needed to do the same.

Waldorf teachers, like good teachers everywhere, make a commitment to the children they teach and work to see their best even when the children try to hide it. They commit themselves and take a chance because the relationship between the teacher and the students is central. When this relationship is built on a teacher's unconditional feeling of concern and responsibility, students prosper. In a Waldorf school this feeling of being responsible for the students is something that teachers take home with them at the end of the day. Many teachers will even think about their students just before they go to sleep, trying to recollect a picture of them at their best. The simple fact that Waldorf teachers care enough to do this consistently can make a big difference.

Imbuing Lessons with Feeling

One of the primary challenges that teachers face in a Waldorf school is the enlivening of everyday subjects by infusing them with emotional content. Subjects such as Astronomy, American History, or Greek Mythology lend themselves to this undertaking, but what about math skills and grammar?

The secret to transforming lessons is in the ability to be imaginative and to understand new ways to introduce a subject. Yet, teachers must also have a feeling for the world that children inhabit and an emotional connection with what they teach. Canadian educator Kieran Egan expresses this clearly in his book, *Imagination in Teaching and Learning,* when he states, "My whole argument is that students are typically imaginatively alive, frequently more imaginatively alive than adults, but that we have allowed curricula and instruction aimed at producing measurable learning to suppress or depress that imaginative activity, at least as far as the content of the curriculum is concerned...But the call on teachers to construct affective images requires primarily that they vivify their own feelings with regard to the subject matter" (Egan, 1992, p. 113). When teachers feel deeply about the subjects they teach, children will respond in kind.

Years ago I taught a grammar lesson on the parts of speech to a third-grade class. To make this subject more child appropriate, I did what Waldorf teachers generally do. I renamed verbs "doing-words" to give the subject immediacy and relevance. I wiped the blackboard completely clean, and I asked the children to tell me some of the things that they could do. Initially, they were slow to respond, as my question puzzled them, but little by little they started to realize what I was looking for. "I run." "I paint." "I sing." "I dance." "I jump...walk ...write...throw." And with each sentence, I would write the verb on the board. Suddenly, one child with a mischievous look on her face said, " I kick." The other children understood her meaning immediately and there was tittering in the class. I simply wrote *kick* on the board and moved on. After a series of other words such as *hike, sing, laugh, sleep,* and *eat,* there came another mischievous contribution, "I punch." Now the children began to snicker again, but I wrote *punch* on the board with the other doing-words. Before long, the entire blackboard was covered with verbs, nearly 100 of them, and it was a visual tribute to all that the children could do, a testimony to the versatility that was being developed in our school.

I run   I sleep   I stand   I paint
I jump   I eat   I whistle I play
I sing   I drink   I shout   I fall
I talk   I think   I dream   I learn
I hop   I sit   I draw   I write
I skip   I walk

Photograph by Jerilyn Ray-Shelley

Then came the real educational moment. The most important aspect of teaching to the feelings of children may well be that every so often a teacher will find him or herself on the threshold of a real life lesson. This happened to me when one of the children asked, "Why are there so many nice words like *sing* and *dance* and *paint* and *smile* and then other words like *kick, punch, hit,* and *spit*?" I was surprised. This simple grammar lesson on verbs had become a lesson on human freedom and responsibility. Here was a chance for the children to learn that in life we really have a choice about what we do.

Infusing Discipline with the Right Feeling

There is usually one area in which teachers do not have trouble responding emotionally, and that is with discipline. Students often find a way to cause even the most placid teachers to respond with strong feelings to their behavior. Although Waldorf teachers are schooled in responding emotionally, anger, impatience, and frustration are not the emotional responses they are seeking.

Steven Levy, a Massachusetts public school teacher and author of *Starting from Scratch*, gives a wonderful example of how a teacher can bring the right feeling to disciplinary situations and achieve the delicate balance that allows a teacher to be a *loving authority.*

> The challenge in discipline is that you have to represent both grace and justice at the same time. The offender has usually acted out of a place of need. She needs to be both inspired, uplifted, strengthened, in confidence. If she is shamed in front of the class, the opposite effect is achieved. On the other hand, the class needs to see that justice has been done, that a crime will not go unpunished. Often I use the secret chamber of the hall to administer the torture.
>
> "Mr. Levy, John keeps shooting a rubber band at me." I put on my stern face. "John, come here right now." We go out in the hall.
>
> The class snickers.
>
> "Ha, he's getting it now."
>
> Meanwhile, out in the hall: "John, whenever we are having a discussion and you raise your hand to speak, I can't wait to hear what you have to say. You bring such an interesting perspective to the class. The class needs your gifts. You are in this class for a special reason and if you do not share your gifts with us, our class will never become what it is supposed to be and neither will you. Do you understand? Now c'mon, we need the best you have to give." John nods his assent. We walk solemnly back into the room. The class believes justice has been done, and John has been encouraged, built up. For many children with a tendency to be disruptive, that is all they need...
>
> I try to administer discipline, in the fourth grade anyway, with a light touch. A bit of humor goes a long way. For example, I have a bell I ring to signal silence. If a child continues talking, I might ask her to provide a meal for the bell, which is obviously weak—since she didn't hear it— and in need of nourishment. The bell feeds on the adoring compliments of its subjects. Some of the most wonderful

writing my children have produced has been letters or poems to the bell. Of course, I read them with great ceremony, and place the bell on the written paper for complete digestion.

[One of Levy's students wrote:]

"Oh Bell, I fear I have fallen into peril, for I have ignored your cry.
I am not worthy,
Oh mightiest of ringers.
Your cry rings over the whole universe, but I do not hear.
Even the deaf can hear you, but not I.
I am your humble servant. Please forgive me! (Levy, 1996, p. 148-151).*

An emotionally responsive teacher will easily become a more creative teacher. When teachers invest themselves emotionally in their teaching, they begin to work out of a deeper part of themselves. They get closer to who they really are and, at the same time, become more authentic and more original. Authenticity and authorship, not authoritarianism, are at the heart of real authority.

The Thoughtful Teacher

The paradox that faces teachers who wish to engage their students on an emotional level is that they must also transform their own thinking. We must counteract the tendency of objectivity to separate us from the world. Parker Palmer, whose work has enabled educators to combine affective and cognitive understandings, writes: "When we distance ourselves from something, it becomes an object; it cannot touch or transform us… Knowing is a human way to seek relationship and, in the process, to have encounters and exchanges that will inevitably alter us" (Palmer, 1998, p. 51-54).

*Reprinted by permission of Heinemann, a division of Reed Esevier, Inc.

As teachers infuse their thinking with imagination, their teaching comes alive. Learning must become an *experience of knowledge,* not just its acquisition. Simple history topics, such as the Great Depression or Roosevelt's New Deal, can be enlivened through a teacher's preparation to become images of people standing in line in front of failed banks, of unemployed workers selling apples and pencils on street corners, of young men leaving their homes to erect cabins and build trails in parks. When presented in this way, children begin to experience what it was like during the 1930's and terms such as the FDIC, the Civilian Conservation Corp, and unemployment insurance take on new meaning. It is through imagination that thinking becomes participatory. Perhaps the most effective way to help children experience another historical era is through drama. Play productions can take students back in time. Costumes and sets give them a feeling for another era and the play itself fills them with understanding.

When teachers activate their thinking in this way, they unite with the subject and, in turn, with their students. Imaginative teaching is one of the basic tenets of Waldorf education. Teachers always need to re-enliven their thinking and to view the subjects that they teach and their students in a new way. To do this effectively, they need to see themselves and let their students see them as *learners,* not simply as *teachers*. They need to model for students a curious, active interest in learning—a willingness to enter into new educational discussions, to consider topics from different perspectives, to find new understandings in everyday experiences, and be willing to teach in a new way, where the learning curve is steep and the risk of failure is pronounced. This is the mark of a good teacher. When they are on the edge and at risk, they are more alert and more alive. This complete presence of mind that is engendered is an essential part of being thoughtfully engaged.

Presence of mind creates a heightened form of awareness and this enables teachers to *read the students* and to respond. When education proceeds in this manner it is a dialogue, a conversation where both teacher and student learn, and where both student and teacher instruct. When teachers are attentive to their students, they can perceive recognition or confusion in students' eyes long before it is too late.

The Reflective Teacher

I have never considered myself a perfect teacher. I love teaching and I love being with children, but I continue to make mistakes. When I assess my work in the light of the three-dimensional paradigm of Waldorf education or in other ways, I invariably find areas where I need to improve. This is one of the ironies of the profession—the more teachers learn, the more they realize there is to know.

Self-evaluation is an integral part of good teaching. My experience has shown me that good teachers can tell you better than anyone else what they do well and where they need to improve. They may not always have the courage to share this information with others, but they will let it leak out to those they trust. A sense of inadequacy is a great gift, as it provides teachers with an opportunity to change and grow.

Teaching as a Path of Self-Development

Demanding work, work that asks for one's best, means change. The more seriously teachers give themselves to their work and reflect on it, the more they can be transformed by the process.

Self-evaluation is an essential part of good teaching. But it is willingness to change and persistent efforts to make change occur that determine how much we actually improve.

In his book, *The Education of the Child,* Rudolf Steiner states that an individual's personal development often takes place on two levels. He notes that there is the change that occurs on the surface, quick change, like the movement of a minute hand on a clock (Steiner, 1996, p. 25). This change takes place in a noticeable way and brings with it new ideas and new terminology, catch phrases, and an alteration in the way that we present our work and ourselves. An example of this is the incorporation of Venn diagrams into lessons or the use of fashionable educational terms such as *honoring* and *rubric*. But more significant changes, changes in habits, temperament, and character, in short, changes in human nature, occur like the movement of the hour hand. These gradual and seemingly imperceptible changes, such as learning to respond to difficult children or difficult parents without becoming defensive, or working to bring order and organization to a chaotic classroom or punctuality to our tendency for tardiness, occur when teachers persevere over an extended period of time. This doesn't mean that teachers become perfect. It simply means that teachers need to continue trying to be better.

Reflective teaching invariably leads to self-knowledge. Although this may sound daunting, there are simple ways to proceed. One understanding is that what makes a teacher good also has within it the possibility of making a teacher ineffective. For instance, classroom management is a skill many teachers need to develop. Getting large numbers of children focused and on task requires a variety of abilities. Teachers have to be clear about directions and expectations, and be both persuasive and compelling. To do this effectively teachers also have to develop a certain degree of insensitivity to individual needs and interests. In moving students from one undertaking to the next, it is often necessary to respond to questions with, "Not now. Please take your seat," or "Tell me about that in a couple of minutes, right now just get started," and of course, "No, you may not change your seat. You need to sit right there." The ability to move a group from one activity to the next requires that teachers ignore certain individual needs.

Some teachers do this so effectively that children simply comply and lessons go smoothly. However, if these teachers do not also cultivate a keen interest in the needs of individual children, their work will suffer. Teachers need simultaneously to have the ability to work with the whole group as well as the ability to focus on the individual. And this balance does not always come easily. Teachers generally start out with a natural inclination in one of these two areas and then realize that they need to work consciously to develop the other.

In his book, *The Lessons of the Hawk,* Mark Kennedy writes that this was a central lesson for his teaching that he learned in a most extraordinary way.

> While out walking recently, I noticed a hawk hunting along the same corridor in which I was travelling. Being in the city, this was a rare treat for me. Stopping to watch him majestically glide to great heights, then swoop in for a better look, was both fun and inspiring. I eventually had to walk on, and as I did, it seemed something deep tugged at the edge of my consciousness; the Hawk had something to teach me about what I had been trying to accomplish with students in my classroom. The full insight didn't present itself on that walk. In fact, it took several months and many more walks, but finally the significance began to penetrate my thinking: the Hawk was at the same time perspicacious and focused. He could see both the whole field and focus on the smallest detail. It is my belief that this understanding can inform our teaching practice (Kennedy, 2001, p. 1).*

Waldorf teachers are encouraged to view education as an art. This sentiment has practical application. Artists invariably use opposites to enhance their work: space and counter space, foreground and background, dark and light, piano and fortissimo, the list is extensive. Similarly, in education teachers must employ opposites to enhance their work. The tension between formality and informality is at the center of classroom

*Reprinted with permission by Holistic Education Press.

discipline. The interplay between staying with prepared lessons and exploring subjects that arise spontaneously gives structure to instruction while at the same time adding life and vibrancy. And when a commitment to high standards is combined with genuine understanding, children and teachers flourish.

Many teachers believe that children need firmness. Yet, an equal number see the opposite just as clearly—that students need love and understanding. Regardless of where teachers begin their educational journey, many eventually adopt a blend of these two understandings, realizing from their classroom experience that children need "loving firmness."

Growing into these new understandings takes time and often happens the hard way through failure. But changes born of failure occur at a deeper level. When experience shows teachers the limits of personal inclination, they begin to recognize the merits in the opposite point of view. This moves them closer to the truth, which is what they should always look for—the truth about themselves and their teaching.

It is out of this feeling of responsibility that Waldorf teachers try to develop in themselves new capacities and new character traits simply for the good of the children. This is what students want and if teachers look carefully they will see confirmation of this in students' eyes when they succeed and when they fail.

If teachers are expecting to help children change, to enable them to overcome certain characteristics, and to develop abilities that complement their natural strengths, they should be willing to be part of the same learning expedition. In fact, they should take the lead.

Discipline begins with self-discipline. A good example of this is found in the following anecdote about Mahatma Gandhi.

The story is told that he was once approached by a mother who had an unusual request concerning her boy, who had a special problem. It seems that the child had difficulty controlling his consumption of sugar and the mother asked Gandhi to speak to the boy and get him to stop. Gandhi agreed, but days passed and still no conversation had taken place. After a week or so, the mother went to Gandhi and expressed her disappointment that nothing had transpired. Gandhi's reply was that before he could speak to the child, he himself had to stop eating sugar (Petrash, 2000, p. 55).

If teachers are concerned about character development in the children they teach, then the teacher's own character development matters. If they want students to learn significant lessons in school, they must be willing to do the same. This may seem like a lot to ask of teachers, but it also underscores the importance of their work. Teachers can make a difference when they give themselves wholeheartedly to the education of children and display a willingness to work on their teaching and themselves. There is an internal aspect to their journey as teachers. Teachers are *inward bound*, so that their work can affect their students on the deepest level.

References

Egan, K. (1992). *Imagination in teaching*. Chicago, IL: University of Chicago Press.

Kennedy, M. (2001). *Lessons from the hawk*. Brandon, VT: Holistic Education Press.

Levy, S. (1996). *Starting from scratch*. Portsmouth, NH: Heinemann.

Palmer, P. J. (1998). *The courage to teach: Exploring the inner landscape of a teacher's life.* San Francisco: Jossey-Bass.

Petrash, J. (2000). *Covering home: Lessons on the art of fathering from the game of baseball*. Beltsville, MD: Robins Lane Press.

Steiner, R. (1996). *The education of the child and early lectures on education (a collection).* Hudson, NY: Anthroposophic Press.

CHAPTER EIGHT

Towards a Truly Human Education

"Our deepest fear is not that we are inadequate. Our deepest fear is that we are powerful beyond measure. It is our light, not our darkness, that frightens us."
—Nelson Mandela

There are gifted teachers all over our country and Dorothy Harrer was one of them. She taught at the Rudolf Steiner School in New York City and made her lessons come alive through the power of imagination.

In a fourth-grade lesson on the study of animals, she asked her students to imagine themselves standing on a craggy precipice halfway up a rocky mountain. As she spoke, the children began to envision a great bird's nest more that six feet in width right at their feet. As the students "looked" into the nest they spotted two downy eaglets waiting for their mother's return. At that moment, the children "heard" the sound of swooping wings and their teacher urged them to step back out of the way as a mother eagle landed.

She then described the mother eagle in detail—the sharp curved beak, the dark perceptive eyes, the white, feathered head, and the sharp talons that held a fish. She explained how the mother reached down with her beak and began to tear off pieces to feed her children. After feeding her young, the mother eagle spread her large wings and was aloft.

 Despite its large size, an eagle weighs only about a dozen pounds and its body contains air-filled pockets. Its feathers are hollow and filled with air, as are its bones, enabling it to soar lightly on the warm updrafts and glide from mountain peak to mountain peak. The children imagined the eagle spiraling higher on the rising air and then as it reached the apex of its flight, falling suddenly to grasp its prey hundreds of feet below.

Although most of these New York City children had never seen an eagle fly in the wild, their minds were alive with the image of this magnificent bird, like the one that was drawn in pastel chalks on their blackboard. They were learning the facts about this bird in a highly effective way, through a picture taking shape in their imaginations. They were beginning to understand the eagle; but they were primed for a deeper lesson. This deeper lesson began when the teacher asked the class, "Children, in what way are you like an eagle?"

The Fullness of Humanity

It was at this point that the children began to learn about themselves as well, about their own humanity and how in their capacity for thinking they have the power to soar like eagles. They can rise with their ideas, and in their imaginations they can travel great distances and look at objects from afar or move in an instant from one point to another with incredible speed. Like the eagle, their thinking also has the ability to focus with great clarity and to see even the smallest detail distinctly. When children see that the admirable characteristics of this great bird are within them, in the power of their thinking, their spirits soar and their self-esteem is bolstered.

This is not an anthropomorphic view of the eagle, but rather an "eagle-ized" view of the human being, one where we sense our kinship with these winged creatures and allow their unique gifts to empower us. This is more in keeping with the Native American's view of the animals in which there is a clear sense that an animal's strength can be conveyed to humans through a sense of kinship and through respect for the spirit of the animal. It is not just with eagles that this link is established in a Waldorf classroom. Lions, cows, mice, deer, even octopi, have something to teach children about what it means to be a human.

When I encountered this lesson, I had one of those "a-ha" experiences, a moment when I realized something that should have been obvious to me long before. Of course, I had known for a long time that Waldorf schools instruct children on a number of different levels. On a basic level, the education provides children with basic skills and good work habits. They

learn to read and write, to calculate and compute, and to complete their work carefully and in a timely fashion.

On another level, the students learn about the world in which they live—about the animals, the plants, the stones, and the stars. They learn about world history, mathematics, literature, art, music, and culture—both today's and yesterday's. Waldorf students receive a classical understanding of human civilization—sometimes a little too European—but a rich one nonetheless, that can easily be expanded to include a greater awareness of Africa and Asia, and Central and South America.

But on a deeper level there is a significant lesson that is taking place, one that has to do with a more central issue—what it means to be a human being. I realized finally, after 20 years of teaching, that this was a fundamental lesson being taught at a Waldorf school, a lesson addressed in so many different ways over the years to help children understand the fullness of their humanity. The schools were designed to help children learn this lesson and it is in this picture of the human being that the spiritual foundation of the school becomes evident.

Preserving Spiritual Connections

One question that is often asked is: "Is a Waldorf school a religious school?" The best answer that I have heard to that question is "Yes and No." It is not a religious school in the way that we commonly think of religion. There is no creed, no catechism, and no proselytizing. Neither are Waldorf schools sectarian, and for that reason they can thrive equally in a Buddhist country such as Japan or on a kibbutz in Israel.

And yet, in a broad and universal way, the Waldorf school is essentially religious. The word religion comes from the Latin root *religare,* which means essentially to re-link. Young children are not yet un-linked from their spiritual connection. A Waldorf preschool teacher's perception of the child is similar to that of the poet William Wordsworth who wrote in his poem, "Intimations of Immortality from Recollections of Early Childhood."

> *There was a time when every meadow grove and stream,*
> *The Earth and all the World did seem,*
> *Appareled in celestial light,*
> *The glory and freshness of a dream.*

This innate spiritual awareness shines in little children like the light that sparkles in their eyes. Jonathan Kozol, the well-known educational reformer, states in his book, *Ordinary Resurrections*, that the unfortunate situation in our country is that "the light is darkened much too soon… in cities all over the nation; and the longing of so many children to reveal their light and bring their goodness to the nation's table is often stifled and obliterated before they are fifteen years old" (Kozol, 2000, p. 42).

For their continued spiritual development, children need only a little outward instruction. According to Rudolf Steiner, they simply need to be taught in a balanced three-dimensional way, one that develops head, heart, and hands to preserve their innate religious awareness.

Although the notion that a balanced education fosters spiritual awareness may seem simplistic, it is based on a theory of knowledge that is at the heart of the Waldorf approach. This understanding is that when feeling and willing—the emotional and volitional aspects of human experience—combine with thinking, children are able to form an inner connection with what they study. This connectedness enables children to live fully in the world and makes it possible for them to find meaning and wonder in existence.

This renewed or enlivened thinking is one of the essential goals of Waldorf education and an important part of what John Gardner tried to convey in his educational writings.

> Thinking that results from (a) change in attitude will not be ordinary thinking… but will begin with empathy and the involvement of soul…It will be feeling that is disciplined and articulated by strict adherence to the qualities of existence that have awakened it. Feeling so directed will eventually coin itself into objective thought, and such deeply grounded thought will be all the more powerful, resonant, and creative…When educators come to a right appreciation of the human capacity of intuitive thought, they will know how to build the bridge between self and world" (Gardner, J., 1996, p. 25-27).

Thinking that is infused with emotional warmth and involvement helps to overcome the dual nature of human experience, marrying the outer and the inner, or the objective and the subjective. Enlivened thinking, the kind of thinking that makes children catch their breath and lean forward with interest, has the power to connect them with the deepest in nature and with the deepest in themselves. In Martin Buber's terminology, it fosters a relationship between the "I" and the world's "Thou." The connection between what lies within the individual and what lies without is so central to Waldorf education that it is underscored each morning when the students begin their day by reciting a morning verse.

> I look into the world in which the sun is shining.
> In which the stars are sparkling
> Where stones in stillness lie,
> Where living plants are growing,
> Where animals live in feeling,
> And where human beings, within their soul, give dwelling
>   to the Spirit.
> I look into the soul that lives within my being—
> The World Creator weaves in sunlight and in soul light,
> In world space there without,

In soul's depths here within.
To Thee, Creator Spirit, I turn my heart to ask
That blessing and pure strength for learning and for work
Should ever flow within me.

—Rudolf Steiner

Teachers must help their students relate with such strong interest to their subjects that they can feel an intimate connection with life and see this relationship as a central part of their human existence. Inner responsiveness counteracts boredom and has a positive influence on a student's experience of the world. According to Rudolf Steiner, the richness of our inner activity influences our ability to enjoy and appreciate life.

(It) is the only key to the beauties of the outer world. It depends upon the inner lives we have developed whether, when we travel across the ocean, only a few inner experiences pass though our souls, or we sense the eternal language of the world spirit and understand the mysterious riddles of creation. The world around us is filled everywhere with the glory of God, but we have to experience the divine in our souls before we can find it in our surroundings" (Steiner, 1994, p. 22, 23).*

*Quotation reprinted with permission by Anthroposophic Press.

Spiritual Well-Being

When a school is based on a spiritual conception of the human being, a more diverse set of values become important. When enlivened thinking is valued, high test scores and scholastic aptitude are seen as partial indicators, limited accomplishments if they are not accompanied by an equal measure of genuine interest and concern for the world.

A boy who I taught for eight years was one of those students for whom academic progress does not come easily. He struggled continually throughout the elementary grades with spelling, punctuation, reading, arithmetic, and more. In spite of this, he was always pleasant, conscientious, and sincere even though he rarely enjoyed the success that other children experienced. Still, his classmates always accepted him and liked him. His teachers invariably found him sweet and considerate and valued his presence in class. Although there were a number of academic lessons that were hard for him, there were lessons that he already had learned about kindness, open-mindedness, and wonder that were often impossible to teach the brightest students.

One day in grade seven we were reviewing the morning's history lesson on the Renaissance. He was writing a composition about Leonardo da Vinci and I was trying to stimulate his memory by recalling some of Leonardo's paintings. I pulled a large art book off the shelf so he could look at one of the paintings that Leonardo had done as an apprentice. It was a painting that demonstrated the artist's unique ability to show the presence of light on an object. When this student looked at the painting and the light on the angel's hair, his mouth opened and his eyes grew wide. He focused in on the curls around the ear, on the strands of hair that looked so lifelike, on the light on each strand and he was visibly moved. He said nothing; he simply took everything in and then began to look at subsequent pages with paintings of the Last Supper and the Mona Lisa. He might not have been able to explain *chiaroscuro*, vanishing points, or foreshadowing, but his appreciation for the work of Leonardo was unmatched. By academic standards, this student was not succeeding in school. His test scores were low, his ability to perform academically was limited. And yet he was conscientious and hardworking. On a heartfelt, human level, he excelled.

At our eighth grade commencement, this young fellow addressed his classmates and the audience and read a piece attributed to an unknown Confederate soldier. When I heard him read the following words, I was moved to tears. This eighth grade graduate clearly had lessons to teach us all.

> *I asked God for strength, that I might achieve.*
> *I was made weak that I might learn humbly to obey.*
> *I asked for health that I might do great things.*
> *I was given infirmity that I might do better things.*
> *I asked for riches that I might be happy.*
> *I was given poverty that I might be wise.*
> *I asked for power that I might have the praise of men.*
> *I was given weakness that I might feel the need of God.*
> *I asked for all things that I might enjoy life.*
> *I was given life that I might enjoy all things.*
> *I got nothing that I asked for, but everything that*
>   *I hoped for.*
> *Almost despite myself, my unspoken prayers were*
>   *answered.*
> *I am among all men most richly blessed.*

The Unspoken Lessons

Sometimes the important spiritual lessons at a school are not actually spoken; they simply are lived. Another of my former students was a young man named David. As a boy he was called "Tito," an affectionate Spanish diminutive, meaning "little one." I also taught Tito for 8 years, from the time he was 6, until he was 14. Our relationship was not always smooth, but we were close.

Tito's parents chose our school for many good reasons, but not because they felt that a child's spiritual development needed to be an important part of an educational program. There were occasions over the years when other students raised spiritual questions, and it was at those times that Tito would occasionally feel himself at odds with his school and his teacher.

This happened once when Tito was about nine years old and his third-grade class was hearing stories from the Hebrew Bible. Creation tales from all over the world are stirring, but the story of Adam and Eve stirred up a whole lot more in Tito than for the other students. One of the students asked a question that students often ask after a story: "Is this story true?" Before I had a chance to answer (and I am really not sure what I would have said) Tito was on his feet. I remember him stating adamantly that he did not believe in Adam and Eve. He said that he had been to the Museum of Natural History and he had seen dinosaurs and he knew that the story of Adam and Eve was not true.

My task was not to convince him to set aside the views on evolution that he had received at home, nor to have him accept on faith the story of creation. My job was to expose him and my other students to these creation stories as I would do in later years with Norse, Egyptian, Indian, and Greek mythology. At the same time that I needed to show respect for each individual child's evolving search for truth, I was to tell the students these stories with reverence and sincerity. Without saying much more, I let the students experience these stories by painting the Days of Creation, by learning words such as *firmament*, *testament*, and *covenant*, and by writing and illustrating the stories of the Garden of Eden, of Abraham and Moses, and David and Goliath in a manner similar to what I would do in subsequent years with the tales of Baldur, Isis and Osiris, and Rama.

Over the years Tito and I had numerous significant discussions. When he graduated from our school, our paths crossed less frequently. But every year or so, he would stop by my house unexpectedly and come in for a visit. We would sit together and reminisce, and he would tell me what he liked about our school and what he didn't. One evening when he was a college student, we sat talking and he said, "I know what the Waldorf School was all about. It's just like you always told us. It was about the importance of balance in our lives." I was surprised. His insight was so clear, but I had never said that. This was an understanding that pervaded our school and one that Tito had absorbed. And it was a lesson that he lived fully in his short life.

Tito died at the age of 26, having done more in an abbreviated time than most people do in 80 years. His life was a testament to balance as can be seen in his obituary below. This was the spiritual lesson he had embraced whole-heartedly. It was something conveyed to him implicitly, not explicitly, through his education. It was brought to him "by the surround, by the insistent influence of the institution itself living out those values" (Sizer, 1984, p. 123).

LORD, MONTAGUE DAVID (Age 26)

David died on Wednesday, August 4, 1993, doing what he wanted to do, in a plane crash crossing the Brooks Range north of Fairbanks, Alaska. "Tito" was artist, cyclist, calligrapher, musician, baseball player, rock-climber, musher, runner, counselor and beloved son. David was a philosopher, outdoorsman, mechanic, dock-builder, archeologist, sign-maker, roofer, bow-maker, pilot and a truly unique free spirit. He is survived by his mother, Anna A. Johnson and fathers, Montague J. Lord and James T. Johnson, Jr., members of the Fearing, Lord and Johnson families, and many close friends. David was born March 2, 1967, in Cleveland, OH, raised in Chevy Chase, MD, graduated from the Washington Waldorf School, Sandy Spring Friends School and Trinity College in Hartford, CT, and homesteaded in Fairbanks, Alaska.

The Spoken Lessons

And yet, there are times when spiritual matters need to be addressed more specifically. When you form a relationship with children and their parents over an extended period of time, as is done in a Waldorf school, you share both the joys and sorrows of life. What does a teacher say to a child when a grandfather dies, or harder still when a mother dies. What does a school say to the children when another student dies? Are they gone or are they near? How do we celebrate a life and express our sadness at the same time? Modest attempts to bring meaning to the tragic events that schools inevitably experience are significant. What a teacher said in the face of the attack on the World Trade Center or the Oklahoma City bombing will matter in the same way that what my English teacher said to our high school class on the day that John F. Kennedy was shot has stayed with me all these years.

Children of various ages need guidance in spiritual matters. Teachers' feeble attempts to shed some light on a difficult subject are important because they let children know that their own spiritual thoughts are of value. At tragic times, Waldorf teachers turn to the same sources that people have turned to all over the world for centuries. Stories, music, inspirational poems and verses, and of course, time for silent reflection, can provide the comfort and solace, as well as the right mood to allow children to find their own answers to life's mysteries. Here is a verse that one of my students once gave me.

> And in the night the heavy Earth is falling,
> From darkness into loneliness, we are falling.
> But there is One who holds that falling,
> Endlessly, gently, in His hands.
> —Rainer Maria Rilke (excerpt from the poem, "Autumn")

Moral Education

Perhaps the greatest amount of discussion concerning the spiritual education of students focuses on moral education. It has become increasingly evident to parents and teachers that moral education must be part of a school's program. According to former U.S. Secretary of Education Bill Bennett, "Here is what we now face in some schools: much cheating, stealing, and in the worst cases violent crimes; acceptance of foul language and talking back to teachers; administrators that are afraid to take a strong moral stand for fear of being sued; too many graduates who believe that there is no such thing as universal moral standards; and more and more children with a cloudy sense of right and wrong" (Bennett, 1999, p. 524). These concerns are shared by many parents, as is the belief that moral education can and should take place in every classroom and every subject.

This is a serious matter for our schools and our society, but also an extremely complicated issue. In his essay "The Education of Character," Martin Buber points out the challenging nature of moral instruction.

> But if I am concerned with the education of character, everything becomes problematic. I try to explain to my pupils that envy is despicable, and at once I feel the secret resistance of those who are poorer than their comrades. I try to explain that it is wicked to bully the weak, and at once I see a suppressed smile on the lips of the strong. I try to explain that lying destroys life, and something frightful happens: the worst habitual liar of the class produces a brilliant essay on the destructive power of lying. I have made the fatal mistake of giving instructions in ethics (Buber, 1965, p. 104).

Trying to help children with moral questions is a comprehensive, three-dimensional undertaking, not simply a matter of "head" learning. It is essential for educators concerned with the spiritual well being of their students to see that moral questions touch the hearts of the children and then manifest in the day-to-day life of the school.

In a Waldorf school, the development of good work habits is part of the moral education that begins with the very first lessons in grade one. In his book, *Education in Search of the Spirit,* John Gardner addresses the topic, "Morality and the Experience of Knowledge" and states:

> [A]ny form of knowledge that fails to elicit a student's whole power of response has important consequences also for their moral development...They (are being) trained not to involve themselves. They have no idea of being called upon either intimately or profoundly. The world passes before their eyes as a moving picture of no very great significance, as something out there that is quite unrelated to the depths of their own souls...The 'I don't care' attitude in moral questions is directly related to the 'I don't care' attitude toward learning. Moral irresponsibility later on is a consequence of psychological unresponsiveness during student days (Gardner, J., 1996, p. 108).*

Moral education can also happen through the stories that are told to children at school. Waldorf teachers would agree with Bill Bennett when he states, "Never underestimate the power of literature to teach good character. Stories and poems can help students see what virtues and vices look like. They offer heroes to emulate. Their moral lessons lodge in the heart and stay there" (Bennett, 1999, p. 536).

Regardless of the religious tradition, stories of individuals who have lived by higher principles inspire and guide students in their own lives. Whether it is the story of the Buddha, Crazy Horse, Mother Theresa, or Nelson Mandela, students will be stirred and guided emotionally by these images. Whether we call the higher principle dharma, conscience, goodness, courage,

*Reprinted with permission by Anthroposophic Press.

love, or compassion, children will see that as human beings they reach their full potential when their ideals are wedded to their day-to-day living.

Out of the stories that touch children's hearts from season to season, out of imaginative thinking that connects children with the world, out of a three-dimensional approach to education there develops a comprehensive understanding of what it means to be a human being. Furthering this idea of the fullness of our humanity is the work of a Waldorf school and of a Waldorf teacher, work that must be continually renewed. Sometimes this renewal will come from inspiring educational readings or from personal meditative reflection, but sometimes it will simply take a teacher by surprise.

It was a warm day in May. A nearly total eclipse of the sun was predicted, but no one was sure that the weather would cooperate. Numerous clouds made the day overcast, but I was a responsible teacher and so I showed my third-grade students how to view the eclipse without looking in the direction of the sun by using a piece of white paper with a very small hole.

The students and I went outside, but the overcast sky made eclipse viewing impossible, or so I thought. About 20 minutes later, the children and I noticed that the sun had come out from behind the clouds. We took out our pieces of paper, exposed our pinholes to the sun and looked down at the eclipse. I would be lying if I said that viewing the eclipse in this way was satisfying.

As we headed toward the school building, the day became beautiful with an eerie polarized light shining on the schoolyard. Some of the children were jumping rope, but several other students were sitting on the blacktop holding baseball caps so that the sun light was shining through the grommet holes and making a ring of crescent suns on the blacktop. Another student was stretching out her mesh vest and dozens of crescent suns were shining beautifully on her lap. I marveled at the ingenuity of the children; their creativity made me feel so old and unimaginative.

As I circled the playground, I passed under a tree. On the ground under the tree were hundreds of little partially eclipsed suns. It seemed that each place where the light was able to filter between the cracks in the leafy canopy, an eclipsed sun became visible on the ground. I was in awe. The thought that came to me was that in some amazing way, each individual ray of light conveyed an image of the sun. In the same way, each individual child bore the image of the divine. There I was standing amidst all of these children, resplendent with divine light in varying degrees of partial eclipse. I could see clearly now their true nature, and the true nature of my work with them, work that was shaped by this spiritual understanding of our humanity.

References

Bennett, W. (1999). ***The educated child: A parents' guide***. New York: Free Press.

Buber, M. (1965). ***Between man and man***. New York: Macmillan.

Gardner, J. F. (1996). ***Education in search of the spirit.*** Hudson, NY: Anthroposophic Press.

Kozol, J. (2000). ***Ordinary resurrections: Children in the years of hope***. New York: Crown.

Sizer, T. (1984). ***Horace's compromise: The dilemma of the American high school***. New York: Houghton Mifflin.

Steiner, R. (1994). ***How to know higher worlds: A modern path to initiation***. (Christopher Bamford, Trans.) Hudson, NY: Anthroposophic Press. (Original work published 1904-1905).

References

Ayers, W. (1993). *To teach: The journey of a teacher*. New York: Teachers College Press.

Bennett, W. (1999). *The educated child: A parents' guide*. New York: Free Press.

Boyer, E. (1983). *High school: A report on secondary education in America*. New York: Harper & Row.

Brookes, G. (1987). *Blacks*. Chicago: Third World Press.

Buber, M. (1965). *Between man and man*. New York: Macmillan.

Cooke, S. (December, 1988). *Reader's digest*. Pleasantville, NY: Reader's Digest Association, Inc.

Cordes, C. & E. Miller. (2000, September 12). *Fool's gold: A critical look at computers in the classroom.* College Park, MD: Alliance for Childhood.

Davey, L.D. (1999). Play and teacher education. In M. Guddemi, T. Jambor, & A. Skrupskelis (Eds.), *Play in a changing society* (p. 42). Little Rock, AR: Southern Early Childhood Association.

DeBrosse, J. (1997, August 4). Schools try longer classes, faster pace. *Chicago Sun Times*, 1B, 4B.

Desmon, S. (2001, December 9). New grade, same teacher. *The Baltimore Sun*, p. A-1.

Egan, K. (1992). *Imagination in teaching*. Chicago, IL: University of Chicago Press.

Eisner, E. (1998). *The kind of schools we need*. Portsmouth, NH: Heinemann.

Foster, N. (May, 1999). How do you choose toys and play materials for the classroom? *In a Nutshell*. Silver Spring, MD: Acorn Hill Children's Center.

Fowler, C. (1996). *Strong arts, strong schools: The promising potential and shortsighted disregard of the arts in American schools*. New York: Oxford University Press.

Gardner, H. (1993). *Frames of mind: The theory of multiple intelligences*. New York: Basic Books.

Gardner, H. (2000). *The disciplined mind: Beyond facts and standardized tests, the K-12 Education that Every Child Deserves.* New York: Penguin Books.

Gardner, J. F. (1996). *Education in search of the spirit.* Hudson, NY: Anthroposophic Press.

Gerwin, D. & L. Harris. (1997). *Genesis of a Waldorf high school: A source book.* Wilton, NH: High Mowing School.

Goral, M. & J. Chlebo. (2000). Where's Waldorf? *Encounter: Education for Meaning and Social Justice*, 13 (3), 43-52.

Hart, L. (1983). *Human brain and human learning.* New York: Longman.

Healy, J. (1990). *Endangered minds: Why children don't think.* New York: Touchstone.

Higgins, J. (1970). *Beyond words: Mystical fancy in children's literature.* New York: Teachers College Press.

Jambor, T. (Fall, 1994). School research and social development. *Dimensions of Early Learning*, p. 17-20.

Jensen, E. (1997). *Teaching with the brain in mind.* Alexandria, VA: ASCD.

Kelly, K. (2000, October 30). Child docs to parents: Stay home and save your kids. *U.S. News and World Report.*

Kennedy, M. (2001). *Lessons from the hawk.* Brandon, VT: Holistic Education Press.

Kozol, J. (2000). *Ordinary resurrections: Children in the years of hope.* New York: Crown.

Krishnamurti, J. (2000). Educating the educator. *Parabola*, 25 (3), 85-89.

Levy, S. (1996). *Starting from scratch.* Portsmouth, NH: Heinemann.

Murray, D. (1996). *Crafting a life in essay, story, poem.* Portsmouth, NH: Heinemann.

National Association of Secondary School Principals. (1996a). *Breaking new ranks: Changing an American institution.* Reston, VA.

National Association of Secondary School Principals. (1996). *Breaking new ranks: Changing an American institution: An executive summary.* Reston, VA.

Palmer, P. J. (1998). *The courage to teach: Exploring the inner landscape of a teacher's life.* San Francisco: Jossey-Bass.

Pearce, J.C. (Fall, 1993).Child's play. *Suncoast Waldorf Association: Teaching as an Art Newsletter*.

Petrash, J. (2000). *Covering home: Lessons on the art of fathering from the game of baseball.* Beltsville, MD: Robins Lane Press.

Pollack, W. (1999). *Real boys: Rescuing our sons from the myths of boyhood*. New York: Henry Holt.

Rogers, C.S. & J.K. Sawyers. (1988). *Play in the lives of children*. Washington, DC: National Association for the Education of Young Children.

Rossi, R. (1999, October 17). Familiar teachers. *Chicago Sun Times*, A-24.

Schwartz, E. (1992). Holistic assessment in the Waldorf school. *Holistic Education Review*, 5 (4), 31-37.

Shore, B. (1999). *The cathedral within: Transforming your life by giving something back.* New York: Random House.

Sizer, T. (1984). *Horace's compromise: The dilemma of the American high school*. New York: Houghton Mifflin.

Smith, B. (1943). *A tree grows in Brooklyn*. New York: Harper Perennial.

Steiner, R. (1994). *How to know higher worlds: A modern path to initiation*. (Christopher Bamford, Trans.) Hudson, NY: Anthroposophic Press. (Original work published 1904-1905).

Steiner, R. (1996). *The education of the child and early lectures on education (a collection).* Hudson, NY: Anthroposophic Press.

Sylwester, R. (1998). Art for the brain's sake. *Educational Leadership* 56 (3), 31-35.

Weinberger, N.M. (1998). The music in our minds. *Educational Leadership* 56 (3), 36-40.

Zernike, K. (2000, October 23). No time for napping in today's kindergarten. *New York Times*, p. A-1.

Index

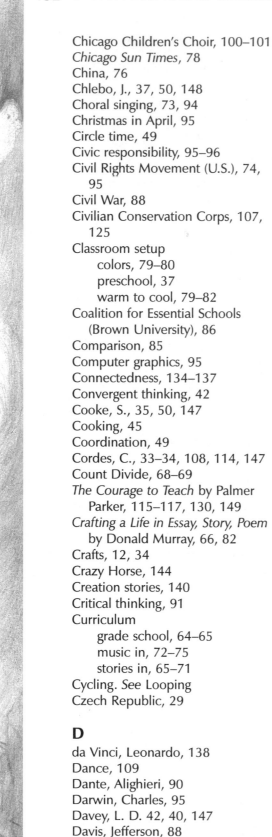

Covering Home

Lessons on the Art of Fathering from the Game of Baseball

Jack Petrash

Writer, father, and baseball fan Jack Petrash combines his love for children with his love for the game of baseball to give fathers meaningful advice on raising children. His message is simple: focus on what you're doing, be in the moment, give yourself to your children the way players give themselves to the game. It's the first book on fathering that mothers will love and fathers will actually read. 160 pages. 2000.

ISBN 1-58904-007-4 / Robins Lane Press / 15932 / HC

The Child and the Machine

How Computers Put Our Children's Education at Risk

Alison Armstrong and Charles Casement

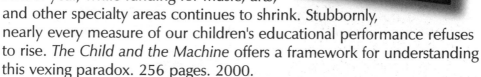

In Los Angeles, the Kittridge Street Elementary School eliminated its music program to hire a technology coordinator. A Virginia school turned its art room into a computer laboratory. In the United States, a record $6.5 billion was spent on educational technology for the 1998-99 school year, while funding for music, arts, and other specialty areas continues to shrink. Stubbornly, nearly every measure of our children's educational performance refuses to rise. *The Child and the Machine* offers a framework for understanding this vexing paradox. 256 pages. 2000.

ISBN 1-58904-005-8 / Robins Lane Press / 13594 / PB

Available at your favorite bookstore, school supply store, or order from Gryphon House at 800.638.0928 or www.gryphonhouse.com.

Creating Rooms of Wonder

Valuing and Displaying Children's Work to Enhance the Learning Process

Carol Seefeldt

What children see around them affects what and how they learn. Displaying children's artwork with thoughtfulness and care benefits children, teachers, and families. Ceilings, floors, tabletops, windows, doors—it's all useful space to display the beautiful works of children, enhance the learning process, and communicate to parents what their children are experiencing in school. Learn how to create rooms of wonder using the basics: color, line, texture, composition, focal points, and rhythm. Then find new ideas for using framing and mounting, boxes, boards, and other materials to value and display children's work. Learn from the theories of Reggio Emilia and put children's art to work! 192 pages.

ISBN 0-87659-265-5 / Gryphon House / 15376 / PB

Early Learning Environments That Work

Rebecca Isbell and Betty Exelby

The classroom environment is a vital part of a child's learning experience. *Early Learning Environments That Work* explores how you can work with furniture, color, materials, storage, lighting, and more to encourage learning through classroom arrangement. Each chapter gives you detailed illustrations and photographs to help you set up or arrange what you already have in the classroom. 192 pages. 2001.

ISBN 0-87659-256-6 / Gryphon House / 14387 / PB

Available at your favorite bookstore, school supply store, or order from Gryphon House at 800.638.0928 or www.gryphonhouse.com.